D1380193

PETER NICHOLS

Peter Nichols was born in Bristol in 1927 and educated at
Bristol Grammar School, Bristol Old Vic Theatre School and
Trent Park Teacher Training College, Herts. His first television
play, *A Walk on the Grass*, was produced in 1959 by the BBC
and among many others which followed were *Promenade*, *Ben
Spray*, *The Hooded Terror*, *The Gorge*, *Hearts and Flowers*
and *The Common*.

His first play for the stage, produced in 1967, was *A Day in
the Death of Joe Egg*, which was roughly based on the half-life
of his firstborn, Abigail, who lived only until she was eleven,
The National Health (RNT), *Forget-Me-Not-Lane* (Apollo and
Greenwich), *Chez Nous* (Globe), *The Freeway* (RNT), *Harding's
Luck*, from E. Nesbit (Greenwich), *Privates on Parade* (RSC),
Born in the Gardens (Bristol Old Vic and the Globe), *Passion
Play* (RSC, 1981), *Poppy* (RSC), *A Piece of My Mind* (Apollo)
and *Blue Murder* (Show of Strength and national tour).
Catch Us If You Can was his first film screenplay, followed
by *Georgy Girl* (co-authored with Margaret Foster, 1966),
Joe Egg, *The National Health* and *Privates on Parade*.

He is the recipient of the John Whiting Award 1967, the
Evening Standard Awards in 1967, 1969, 1978 and 1982, the
Society of West End Theatre Awards in 1978 and 1982, and
the Ivor Novello Award for Best Musical for *Poppy* (1985).
A Day in the Death of Joe Egg won two Tony Awards when
it was revived on Broadway in 1985. He has directed revivals
and premières of six of his plays. He is a Fellow of the Royal
Society of Literature.

A memoir, *Feeling You're Behind*, came out in 1984, his forty
or so diaries are in the theatre archives of the British Library,
and a selection is to be published in a volume by Nick Hern
Books under the title *Diaries 1969–77*. He is currently working
on a musical based on the music of Hoagy Carmichael as well
as a new stage play, *So Long Life*, which was broadcast on
Radio 4 in 2000 and is to be staged in Bristol later in the year
by Show of Strength profit-sharing company. The Gulbenkian
Foundation have invited him to write a play about genetic
engineering.

By the Same Author

Stage plays

A Day in the Death of Joe Egg
The National Health
Forget-Me-Not Lane
Chez Nous
The Freeway
Privates on Parade
Born in the Gardens
Poppy
A Piece of My Mind
Blue Murder
So Long Life (*forthcoming*)

Television plays

Promenade (in *Six Granada Plays*)
Ben Spray (in *New Granada Plays*)
The Gorge (in *The Television Dramatist*)

Autobiography

Feeling You're Behind
Diaries 1969-77 (*forthcoming*)

PETER NICHOLS

Passion Play

NICK HERN BOOKS
London
www.nickhernbooks.co.uk

A Nick Hern Book

Passion Play first published as a paperback original
in this revised edition in 2000 by Nick Hern Books Limited,
14 Larden Road, London W3 7ST

Passion Play first published in Great Britain in 1981
Passion Play copyright © Peter Nichols 1981, 1985, 2000
Afterword copyright © Peter Nichols 2000

Peter Nichols has asserted his right to be identified as
the author of this work

Passion Play is published by arrangement with Methuen Publishing

Front cover image from Allen Jones's *Magician Suite, 1976*
(lithograph), reproduced with permission

Typeset by Country Setting, Kingsdown, Kent CT14 8ES
Printed by Biddles, Guildford

A CIP catalogue record for this book is available from
the British Library

ISBN 1 85459 605 5

Passion Play was first staged by the Royal Shakespeare Company at the Aldwych Theatre, London, on 8 January 1981, directed by Mike Ockrent, with Louise Jameson (Kate), Benjamin Whitrow (James), Billie Whitelaw (Eleanor), Priscilla Morgan (Agnes), Anton Rodgers (Jim) and Eileen Atkins (Nell).

Retitled *Passion*, its New York premiere was at the Longacre Theatre on 15 May 1983, directed by Marshall W. Mason, with Roxanne Hart (Kate), Bob Gunton (James), Cathryn Damon (Eleanor), Stephanie Gordon (Agnes), Frank Langella (Jim) and E. Katherine Kerr (Nell).

Passion Play was revived at the Haymarket, Leicester, on 8 March 1984, transferring to Wyndham's Theatre London on 18 April 1984, directed by Mike Ockrent, with Heather Wright (Kate), Leslie Phillips (James), Judy Parfitt (Eleanor), Patricia Heneghan (Agnes), Barry Foster (Jim) and Zena Walker (Nell).

Passion Play was revived again, in the version published here, at Donmar Warehouse on 13 April 2000 with the following cast:

KATE	Nicola Walker
JAMES	James Laurenson
ELEANOR	Cherie Lunghi
AGNES	Gillian Barge
JIM	Martin Jarvis
NELL	Cheryl Campbell

Other parts were played by Ruth Brennan, Toni Kanal, Arthur Kelly, Francis Maguire and Peter Winnall.

Directed by Michael Grandage
Designed by Christopher Oram
Lighting by Hartley T.A. Kemp
Sound by Fergus O'Hare (for Aura)

This production transferred to the Comedy Theatre, London, on 21 June 2000 with the same cast, except that Jim was now played by Nicky Henson and other parts by Heather Craney, Judith Hepburn, Tom Marshall and Katherine Spark.

Characters

KATE, 25

JAMES, 50

ELEANOR, 45

AGNES, 50

JIM, 50

NELL, 45

A number of other actors (six if possible) who do not speak written dialogue. They play waiters, a doctor, diners, guests and critics at private views, shop assistants, etc.

ACT ONE

A living room.

ELEANOR, JAMES *and* KATE *are seated, drinking from coffee cups and glasses.* KATE *is smoking. Someone has just finished speaking.*

Silence. KATE *puts out her cigarette.* JAMES *breathes in sharply, covers his mouth.* ELEANOR *drains her glass. A clock chimes the first half.*

KATE. What's that? Midnight already?

JAMES. Half past.

KATE. No! My watch must have stopped. Christ. Sorry.

ELEANOR. Whatever for?

KATE. I'd no idea. No wonder James was yawning.

JAMES. Was I?

ELEANOR. He's always yawning.

KATE. I must go.

JAMES. At my age I nod off so easily.

ELEANOR. At your age? You've always been a yawner.

JAMES. A yawner possibly.

ELEANOR. All our married life.

JAMES. I've never been in the habit of nodding off before. Not like now, at the drop of a hat.

ELEANOR. You've always needed at least eight hours.

JAMES. There's no place like bed.

KATE. Right.

ELEANOR. We're all agreed on that.

KATE. And I must let you get to yours. I didn't mean to stay so long.

ELEANOR. You're mad. We love people dropping in.

KATE. In that case I'll come more often.

ELEANOR. We'd love that. Wouldn't we James?

JAMES (*yawning*). Absolutely. Forgive me.

KATE. And thanks for offering to help with my book. It was your stories of the Arab sheikhs and their art collections gave me the idea in the first place.

JAMES. I'll be what use I can. Which isn't much, I'm afraid. Strictly Restoration.

ELEANOR. You've helped them buy the right pictures too.

JAMES. Only as a sideline.

KATE. Almost the last thing Albert did was get the publishers to commission this book.

ELEANOR. You must finish. You owe it to him.

KATE. Right. And I still haven't thanked you for helping me so much over his death and the funeral. Letting me cry on your shoulders.

ELEANOR. We all had a good cry. He was such an old friend.

KATE. You knew him even before his marriage.

JAMES. I knew him before you were born.

KATE. And yet, when he came to live with me, you accepted that too. That can't have been easy knowing Agnes as well as you did.

ELEANOR. Divided loyalties. Always tricky. But you were so obviously fond of him.

JAMES. And he of you. That's what Agnes couldn't forgive.

KATE. Still can't.

JAMES. No?

KATE. She seemed fine at the funeral but since then all the bad blood's gathered again.

JAMES *yawns. She stops.*

Why struggle, James? Just let it come.

JAMES. God. I'm sorry.

KATE (*kisses him*). Bye bye.

JAMES. I'll send you on a list of names.

KATE. Great. Really. And sometime soon an hour's chat with a tape recorder? Both of you?

ELEANOR. We're almost always here. You know our number.

KATE. Right.

ELEANOR *and* KATE *go to the hall.* JAMES *stays in the room, clearing glasses and putting* KATE's *empty cigarette packet in the ashtray.*

ELEANOR *and* KATE *stay in the hall.* ELEANOR *helps* KATE *on with outdoor clothing. They talk, but their dialogue is drowned by a sudden fortissimo burst of choral music. Mozart's Requiem: from 'Dies Irae' to 'Stricte Discussurus'.*

By the time it's over, KATE *has gone to the front door and* ELEANOR *has returned to* JAMES *in the living room. The music ends as suddenly as it began.*

JAMES. I thought she'd never go.

ELEANOR. That was obvious.

JAMES. Well, nearly quarter to one –

ELEANOR. I'd be in no hurry either. Back to an empty flat, a lonely bed. He died so suddenly. I don't know how she can stay on there, with so many memories of Albert.

JAMES. Could it be because *she's* not much more than a memory of Albert? She's got his phrases, gestures, points of view. Like a ghost!

ELEANOR. What chance has she had to be anything else?
Five years with Albert *I'd* be a ghost.

JAMES. I doubt it. She was no-one to *start* with.

ELEANOR. I happen to like her.

JAMES. I don't *mind* her.

ELEANOR. You made her feel about this small.

JAMES. How d'you know what she felt?

ELEANOR. She told me.

JAMES. No.

ELEANOR. In the hall, just now. I think you might have made
an effort.

JAMES. I *was* making an effort.

ELEANOR. It cost her a lot to ask that favour but you left her
feeling about this small.

JAMES. As you said before.

ELEANOR. Why is it you never like my girlfriends?

JAMES. Kate's one of your girlfriends, is she?

ELEANOR. Why not?

JAMES. Isn't she a bit young?

ELEANOR. I enjoy young people's company.

JAMES. She's about the same age as our daughters.

ELEANOR. Same as Janet, older than Ruth.

JAMES. And you didn't crave *their* company.

ELEANOR. I *enjoyed* it. Anyway, Ruth and Janet have gone
now, they've got their husbands to look to. And daughters
are different. I'm not Kate's mother.

JAMES. You're old enough to be.

ELEANOR. I talk to her in a way I never could with the girls.

JAMES. Really? What about?

ELEANOR. Men. Sex. Love. She very much reminds me of myself when I was her age.

JAMES. Seriously?

ELEANOR. Can't you see the resemblance?

JAMES. You were a working-class dropout on the run from a provincial suburb. Kate's a stockbroker's daughter, well-heeled, knows the score –

ELEANOR. That doesn't matter. We're both looking for a brighter world; we go for the same kind of men –

JAMES. Albert?

ELEANOR. Not Albert. You. (*He looks at her.*) She told me when we went to make the coffee. She finds you a very attractive man. So there's your chance.

JAMES. If only I found her an attractive woman.

ELEANOR. You make it very obvious you don't. Which must be quite a challenge to a girl like that.

JAMES. Then *you* don't think she *does* find me attractive?

ELEANOR. I'm sure she does. She means nothing by it, though. Otherwise why tell *me*?

JAMES. She wants to flatter me into helping her with this dreary book.

ELEANOR. But I was clearly meant to pass it on, so I have.

JAMES. Very generous.

ELEANOR. I like to see you happy.

JAMES. Knowing she doesn't interest me.

ELEANOR. Even if she did, an approach like that would only send you pelting for cover.

She leaves the room with the glasses, etc. She goes through the kitchen and off, he following her, calling:

JAMES. Don't be too sure! The right offer on the right day, from the right woman, I've already warned you, someone with my lack of experience would be mad not to grab with both hands.

He bolts the front door. She returns and they move through the hall together towards the stairs.

ELEANOR. I'm sick of hearing this. You had as much as most men. Certainly as many chances.

JAMES. In our day you could never be sure. Girls' behaviour then was criminal. There was so little action, it's a wonder the race survived.

ELEANOR. Quite a few girls tried the direct approach with you.

JAMES. *You* never tried the direct approach.

ELEANOR. I learnt from watching the other girls fail. They scared you off. I wanted you to come to me.

JAMES. You could afford to. (*He embraces and kisses her.*) You were the most attractive. Still are.

She avoids his advances and starts to climb the stairs.

No amount of coming out with it could ever be match for you. Sitting there like a cat with cream. Smug's the word for that. (*He catches up and begins making love.*) Aren't you, eh, a cat with cream?

ELEANOR. What *are* you doing?

JAMES. Smug as hell. A girl like Kate can tell *you* I interest her because, of course, she knows she's safe. She knows I'm yawning for her to leave so that you and I can be alone.

ELEANOR. What, here?

JAMES. Why not? Now the girls have gone? We're all alone. No-one's going to appear on the landing and ask us what we are doing. Why I'm hurting Mummy.

ELEANOR. It's many a year since they did that.

JAMES. And many a year since we did this.

ELEANOR. You *are* hurting Mummy. You'll put my back out.

JAMES. The top stair then. With the flat landing?

ELEANOR. James! I'm a grandmother. You're a grandfather. There's a place for that kind of thing. (*She frees herself.*) It's called the bedroom.

She climbs to the top, opens the door there and goes off by it. He follows, turns off all the lights and goes off too, closing the door.

The 'Dies Irae' bursts out again.

A restaurant.

KATE sits alone, smoking with a drink. Behind her, a table where two WOMEN sit talking and drinking coffee.

A WAITER replaces KATE's drink with another, smiles at her, speaks. She thanks him, finishes the last and hands him the glass. He leans over and speaks. She listens, smiling. The WAITER leads her to a vacated table and she sits. He lays a napkin on her lap. JAMES arrives and the music ends.

KATE. Hullo.

JAMES. God, I'm sorry.

KATE. Don't be.

He sits beside her. Mutter of conversation and sounds of knives and forks.

JAMES. I thought you'd be gone. This Lebanese curator talks the hind legs off a donkey.

KATE. It's all right.

JAMES. I thought –

KATE. You're here. That's all that matters. (*Offers her cheek to be kissed. He does.*) I'd already scored with the waiter.

JAMES. You've got a drink.

KATE. My third.

The WAITER approaches, stands by.

JAMES. I'm usually so punctual.

KATE. I'm not. I warn you. Just today. Serves me right for being too eager.

JAMES. Cinzano Bianco, please.

The WAITER *goes.* JAMES *looks at the menu.*

Have you ordered anything to eat?

KATE. I can't think about food. Too excited. Too many butterflies. It's been like that ever since you called.

JAMES. That seems disproportionate. I only wanted to suggest some other people you might interview for your book.

KATE. Is that all? I thought perhaps you had received my message?

JAMES. Message?

KATE. I sent a message through your wife. She didn't pass it on?

JAMES. I don't think so.

KATE. Unexpected. (*She shrugs*). She can't be as confident as she looks.

JAMES. Oh. If you mean being *fond* of me – ?

KATE. Finding you attractive.

JAMES. That's it, yes, she told me that, yes, very flattering for a man of my age. Yes, she did. Thanks.

KATE. I like older men.

JAMES. Well, obviously. Albert was my age exactly.

KATE. D'you know he admired you more than anyone?

JAMES. That much? We were close friends certainly, over thirty years, but he had such a brilliant career, all get-up-and-go, by comparison I must have seemed a stick.

KATE. One of his strengths as an editor was he recognised the real stuff when he saw it. He made me watch you closely.

Your modesty fascinated him. *The* man in his field, he used to say, no contenders.

JAMES. Well, restoring modern art is not that wide a field, you know. More like a kitchen garden.

KATE. Albert said: Watch my friend James. Never shows off. Doesn't need to. That's a man in total control of himself. Nobody's ever disturbed his equilibrium. Watch him closely. So I did.

The WAITER *returns with* JAMES*'s drink, sets it before him, leaning over.* KATE *does not alter her voice.*

And that's how I came to realise you're one of the most desirable men I've ever met.

JAMES *looks up at the* WAITER.

JAMES. Thank you.

KATE. Almost painfully so. You must have noticed –

JAMES. Would you like some vichyssoise? Gaspacho? A little salmon?

KATE. Anything light. I don't mind.

JAMES (*ordering*).Two vichyssoise, fresh salmon for the lady, and for me escallopes provencales. (*To* KATE.) And to drink? Soave, Valpolicella? (*She shrugs.*) Soave.

The WAITER *writes and goes with the menus.*

KATE. I'm sorry if my interest was ever an embarrassment.

JAMES. Never. No. Except perhaps with that waiter –

KATE. It must have been so obvious at times. Though I tried not to let it show.

JAMES. I honestly didn't notice.

KATE. Come on –

JAMES. Never occurred to me.

KATE. Amazing.

JAMES. You were Albert's girl. Taboo.

KATE. Right. I didn't dare move while he was alive and as we never met without your wife I thought the best approach was through her.

JAMES. Eleanor assumed you only flattered me to use my connections. Luckily.

KATE. She was meant to.

JAMES. I did myself.

KATE. Ah. My cover-up was *too* effective.

JAMES. Do myself, I must admit.

KATE (*Her hand on his*). Forget that now.

JAMES. The only time I thought of you like that was at his funeral.

KATE. I *chose* that dress for you.

JAMES. Dress?

KATE. Purple silk. Cost the earth.

JAMES. I didn't notice the dress. No, I meant that suddenly seeing you as Albert's what shall I call you – common-law widow?

KATE. Right.

JAMES. Among his middle-aged friends, I realised how young you were. And I couldn't help but see the way some of Albert's mates consoled you.

KATE. Right! The friends who'd been the last to accept me as his lover were the first to try to undress me as his widow.

JAMES. I remarked on that to Eleanor.

KATE. I didn't *mind*. Being suddenly available is quite arousing. The ultimate sexual threat. The other wives were very much aware. And I knew *you* were watching. Which was nice too.

JAMES. I wasn't watching. I *noticed*.

She smiles, finishes her gin. The WAITER *serves food.*

The light fades slightly on the restaurant set and comes up fully on the living room where ELEANOR *enters from the kitchen door with* AGNES. *They go into the living room, bringing mugs of coffee.*

AGNES. You noticed that, did you?

ELEANOR. Not till James remarked on it.

AGNES. Their hands were everywhere. God Almighty, I thought, you smutty little trollop.

ELEANOR. I'm not sure you can blame Kate for that.

AGNES. I can blame her for wearing a purple silk creation that must have cost my husband more than he ever spent on a dress for me. And scent you could have cut with a scythe. I blame her for rushing along that very morning to have an expensive hair-do.

ELEANOR. You don't *know* that, Agnes.

AGNES. I know how it looks without, my dear.

ELEANOR. She was only being the good hostess. Which is what she's chiefly known for.

AGNES. What she's chiefly known for is stealing other people's husbands.

ELEANOR. Only once.

AGNES. Once! You don't imagine that was the first time those old mates had felt her up?

ELEANOR. I thought so, yes.

AGNES. She might at least have fought off their drunken fingers till after the funeral. With our sons and daughters there and Albert's relatives –

ELEANOR. Kate's people didn't come?

AGNES. They've never approved. Her father didn't relish the thought of a son-in-law older than himself. Calling him 'Dad'.

The lights favour JAMES *and* KATE.

KATE. I can't manage any more.

JAMES. You've eaten nothing.

KATE. My heart's in my mouth. I can hardly breathe. Can you?

JAMES. Shall I order coffee?

KATE. No. There's coffee at my place.

JAMES. That's out of the question, Kate. There's a painting I told Eleanor I must leave in Bond Street and as you know my home's half an hour's drive at least from there –

KATE. I can do it in fifteen minutes.

JAMES. I remember your driving, yes.

KATE. I didn't mean the drive. (*She takes his hand and kisses it.*)

JAMES. She'll wonder where I've been.

KATE. So she doesn't know we're meeting?

JAMES. I told her I'd be eating with the Lebanese curator –

KATE. Two alibis? Not clever. It looks fishy. You get sussed out.

JAMES. But I could say I'd met you and given you a few more names.

He hands her an envelope.

KATE. Three alibis? And you didn't know I was interested? Well it's all true so far.

JAMES. Would you rather she knew? You don't care?

KATE (*shrugs*). Why should I, if you can't come back for coffee?

JAMES. I'll probably tell her then.

KATE. Do.

JAMES. D'you want coffee here?

KATE. Mine's better.

JAMES. I'm sure.

KATE. I may have some alone, thinking of you. But it won't be the same.

JAMES *beckons the* WAITER.

In the living room, ELEANOR *is still moving and* AGNES *is still.*

ELEANOR. I hesitate to say this, Agnes, but if close friends can't, who can? I'm sorry to hear you still going on, that's all.

AGNES. Going on?

ELEANOR. About Albert and Kate. I'd hoped now he's dead, you'd find the generosity to forget what happened. Well, forgive anyway. Your friend's such a pleasant man, your life's taken a fresh direction –

Pause. She looks straight at AGNES, *who pointedly waits as though for the end of a sermon.*

AGNES. My new friend and I have both been through the wars and without each other we might never have picked up the pieces again. But what makes you believe he could ever in a million years make up for the loss of my husband? And I don't mean his death, I mean the loss while he was alive! Haven't you even grasped that Albert was my life? We not only had four children, we made his career. Together. Coming from a semi-literate home, he rose to become a crusading editor: he influenced the finest minds in his generation. And finally threw all that away to satisfy an itching cock.

ELEANOR. Well, not entirely, Agnes –

AGNES. Then you tell me to forgive and forget?

ELEANOR. I mean, he did continue to function after he went to live with Kate –

AGNES. Forgive that bitch? What for?

ELEANOR. For *your* sake. Your peace of mind.

JAMES *has paid the bill and he and* KATE *are leaving their table and making across the upper level to the stairs. The* WAITER *clears, light goes out on him.*

AGNES. Don't waste your sympathy on me, dear. I've got a little man takes care of that.

ELEANOR. Then for the sake of your friends –

AGNES. What friends?

ELEANOR. *We're* still your friends.

AGNES. James never liked me.

ELEANOR. Not true. And we none of us like seeing you in this bitter state –

AGNES. Oh, don't you like it? Oh, how sad!

ELEANOR. It's boring to listen to, frankly.

AGNES. It doesn't bore me. Christ, no! It keeps me alive. I'll see her in the poorhouse. Though perhaps the whorehouse would suit her better.

JAMES *and* KATE *have come down the stairs and turn into the hall space.*

KATE. Thanks for lunch, if nothing else.

JAMES. Thank you for coming.

AGNES. I'll take back everything he gave her.

KATE. You must taste *my* coffee some time.

AGNES. Every lemon squeezer.

KATE. Some time soon.

AGNES. Everything she didn't buy.

JAMES. I'd like that, yes, but I can't often get away.

KATE. It's time you did.

AGNES (*smiling*). He never married her, did he?

JAMES. Perhaps it is.

KATE *stands close, pressing her body against his.*

ELEANOR. Kate wouldn't have him. She values her freedom.

AGNES. I'll fight her till I drop.

KATE. Please try, won't you?

ELEANOR. You'll lose your friends.

AGNES. I can manage without.

JAMES (*calling*). Taxi!

KATE. You know where I am. Just ring.

She kisses JAMES *on the mouth, lingeringly.*

AGNES. This is more important than pleasing friends. This is fighting evil, Eleanor, which Albert did too as long as he could spot it.

The kiss ends.

KATE. Next time we'll have the coffee first. Only eat when we've worked up an appetite.

She turns to go.

JAMES. I'll give your love to Eleanor.

He goes off the other way.

AGNES. You can only tell me to forgive because you haven't the vaguest idea how this experience *feels.*

ELEANOR. I suppose that's true. James and I have been unusually lucky. Our daughters used to complain we were getting dull.

AGNES. Well –

ELEANOR. Really?

AGNES. A bit.

ELEANOR. D'you think so?

AGNES. You never surprise us.

ELEANOR. Sometimes we'd have welcomed a dash of danger.

AGNES. It's how to stop it once you've started. I was tolerant to start with. I thought that was the best way to deal with it.

ELEANOR. Perhaps James and I are a naturally monogamous pair.

AGNES. Who isn't? Who doesn't believe it's made in Heaven?

ELEANOR. We don't think *that*. We're not romantic. My opinion is most couples come to grief through expecting too much of each other.

The front door opens and JAMES *enters.*

Oh, hullo love. Where on earth have you been till now?

JIM *enters at the cupboard, dressed the same as* JAMES. *No one acknowledges him.*

JIM. The traffic. We agreed the traffic.

JAMES. The traffic.

AGNES. Oh, God, is it bad?

JAMES. Friday afternoon? Agnes! How good to see you! I was afraid you might have gone.

AGNES. I'm on my way.

They kiss. ELEANOR *stands by.*

You smell sexy. Nice aftershave.

JAMES. Why are you rushing off like this?

AGNES. I'm meeting my fellow at half-past three and isn't it getting on for that now?

JAMES. Ten past.

AGNES. Must dash. Bye-bye.

ELEANOR. Let's go shopping some time, shall we?

They kiss. The men watch.

JIM. Better *tell* her. I want to tell her.

AGNES. I don't get that much time.

JIM. After Saint Agnes goes.

ELEANOR. Just an hour or two.

JIM. I *want* to tell her.

AGNES. I'll try.

JIM. Not everything.

AGNES. Goodbye James.

JAMES. Bye-bye.

> AGNES *goes.*

> ELEANOR *closes the door.*

JIM. Not about the kiss, for instance.

ELEANOR. Hullo, my love.

> *She embraces and kisses him.*

JIM. In the restaurant, the whole length of her body against mine –

ELEANOR. I've missed you.

JAMES. Have you?

JIM. – her tongue straight to the back of my mouth, circling like a snake inside –

ELEANOR. Haven't you missed me?

JAMES. I always miss you.

JIM. The almost forgotten feel of an unknown woman –

ELEANOR. Agnes was right. You reek of perfume –

JIM. Christ!

JAMES. Do I?

ELEANOR. *Is* it aftershave?

JIM. She *knows* your aftershave!

ELEANOR. I don't think so.

JAMES. I've no idea.

ELEANOR. Smells more like women's perfume.

JIM. The dealer. Magda.

JAMES. Oh, in the gallery, yes, this dragon was wearing some kind of knockout drops, I remember.

ELEANOR. It *smells* like Bond Street.

JAMES. What does Bond Street smell like?

ELEANOR. Expensive tarts.

JAMES. What do you know about expensive tarts?

ELEANOR. Not a lot.

JAMES. They liked my work on the painting.

ELEANOR. Which was that?

JAMES. The Frank Stella.

ELEANOR. They must have kept you hanging about.

They have now returned to the living room.

JIM. No. She can easily catch you out there.

JAMES. Not long, no.

JIM. Talk more. You usually talk more, don't you? Simply say you had some lunch with Kate, gave her the list of names and –

ELEANOR. Did you have a drink at the gallery?

JAMES. No!

ELEANOR. Not white wine? You haven't drunk white wine?

JAMES. No.

ELEANOR. I thought I tasted it when you kissed me.

JIM. Lunch.

JAMES. That was lunch.

JIM. With Kate.

JAMES. With the Lebanese curator.

JIM. Kate!

JAMES. He wants me to buy more post-impressionists for his sheikhs.

JIM. And you met Kate for a drink nearby –

JAMES. It's a profitable sideline buying for the Gulf.

ELEANOR. Yes, indeed.

JIM. Why are you doing this? To hide the fact that you've eaten lunch with an attractive girl who doesn't attract you?

ELEANOR. Arabs don't drink, do they?

JIM. Christ! Orange!

JAMES. Orange juice. I had the wine.

JIM. Still not too late to say you met for a drink –

JAMES. Agnes looked rather well, I thought.

ELEANOR. We had a nasty scene.

JAMES. Oh, dear.

He is absently moving about. She is correcting a score.

JIM. But you're right, she wouldn't understand –

ELEANOR. If you'd been sooner, it wouldn't have happened.

JAMES. Sorry about that.

JIM. And anyway you don't *want* to tell her. Don't want it to finish there, do you?

JAMES. What was your disagreement about?

JIM. You feel alive.

ELEANOR. Oh, Kate, Kate, Kate, what else?

JIM (*to her*). I've just had lunch with Kate.

ELEANOR. She never talks of anything else.

JIM. Except that neither of us could eat.

ELEANOR. And I'm afraid I told her so.

JIM. Her tongue's been in my mouth.

ELEANOR. I told her it was boring.

JAMES. No wonder you had a disagreement.

JIM. She's not pretty, Eleanor.

ELEANOR. Well, she was so vindictive to Kate.

JIM. Not nearly as pretty as you.

JAMES. Even now that Albert's dead?

JIM. But different. More flagrant.

JAMES. What can she do?

JIM. Kate doesn't care who's watching.

ELEANOR. She wants everything back. Every single thing he bought her. I found myself defending Kate. I've decided I like her better.

JIM (*to her*). I love you, Eleanor. But she's exciting.

JAMES. Should we warn her, d'you think?

JIM. She's dangerous.

ELEANOR. She can look after herself.

JAMES. Absolutely.

JIM. Anyone could have seen that kiss.

ELEANOR. Intruders get caught in the crossfire.

JIM. Though I suppose it wouldn't *look* much to a passer-by.

JAMES. D'you feel like a little nap?

JIM. An affectionate goodbye at most.

JAMES (*embracing her*). An afternoon lie-down?

JIM. No more.

ELEANOR. I'm giving a lesson in fifteen minutes.

JIM. A passer-by couldn't have seen the tongue.

JAMES. How long for?

ELEANOR. An hour.

JAMES. And then?

ELEANOR. And then we're rehearsing Verdi's *Requiem* for the Albert Hall and what you call a little nap requires a long nap afterwards.

She has her score and moves to the hall, JAMES *and* JIM *following.*

I don't want to repeat the occasion I was singled out from the other sopranos for yawning in the Sanctus. How about tonight?

JAMES. You know very well afternoons are best.

ELEANOR. Tomorrow afternoon then.

JAMES. Alright. Tonight.

ELEANOR (*laughing*). Whatever's the matter with you suddenly? While I'm teaching have a cold bath. Or go for a run.

JAMES. I might do that.

She takes the score off to the music room upstage of the living room. JAMES *stays in the hall.* JIM *goes to the cubicle representing a phone booth; he dials, waits.* JAMES *calls off to* ELEANOR.

JAMES. Are you sure you're free tomorrow afternoon?

Lights up on KATE's *room. Couch, chair, low lighting. A phone on the floor is ringing.* KATE *enters, wearing only a slip-on gown, smoking a cigarette. She kneels to answer.* JIM *puts his money in. Sounds of the tone until he does.* ELEANOR *comes from the music room.*

ELEANOR. What?

JAMES. Are you free tomorrow afternoon?

ELEANOR. One student in the morning. Afternoon quite free.

KATE. Yeah?

JIM. Hullo? Kate?

KATE. Yeah.

JIM. James Croxley here.

KATE. Hullo.

ELEANOR. Shall I book you in? (*She goes to the foot of the stairs.*)

KATE. How are you? (*She lies on the couch, resting the receiver on her stomach.*)

JAMES. And no choir rehearsal?

ELEANOR. Not till Saturday.

JIM. I was a bit late home and Eleanor wondered where I'd been.

JAMES. I'll keep you to that.

KATE. So you told her. What did she say?

JIM. I didn't, no –

KATE. I see –

JIM. Well, Agnes was there and I thought –

KATE. Agnes? She'd have suspected all kinds of wild things that I'm sad to say never happened.

ELEANOR (*to* JAMES, *who is following her up the stairs*). Where are you going now?

JIM. Yes.

JAMES. To put my running shoes on.

JIM. And wasted no time suggesting them to Eleanor.

KATE. Right. A very heavy scene.

ELEANOR. Are you coming to Saturday's concert?

JAMES. Isn't it being broadcast live?

ELEANOR. Yes.

JIM. They both smelt your perfume on me.

KATE. Poor James.

JAMES. I'll listen at home. You won't mind?

She precedes him into the bedroom. He shuts the door behind them.

KATE. What did you say? About the perfume?

JIM. I said it was someone else's.

KATE. Someone else's?

JIM. The Bond Street dealer's.

KATE. I suppose you're pretty nifty on your feet.

JIM. How d'you mean?

KATE. Used to dealing with narrow scrapes?

JIM. Not at all.

KATE. Did she believe you?

JIM. Yes, I think so. I was going to say I'd lunched with you but by the time Agnes had gone, the moment seemed to have passed. So can I ask you not to mention it?

KATE. I wasn't going to.

JIM. No, I'm sure.

KATE. You sound as breathless as I feel.

JIM. I've been jogging round the common. I've no more coins so I can't talk long. There's something you should be warned about. Would you care to come to dinner with us, here? Next week.

KATE. Warned about? What?

JIM. Otherwise on Saturday night, if you're not busy I could drop in at your place

The 'Agnus Dei' from Mozart's Requiem, sudden and loud.

JIM and KATE continue for some moments unheard, then lights fade on JIM as he replaces the telephone. KATE puts hers down too and continues lying on the settee, smoking.

The lights change on her room to show more. JAMES
*enters, wearing shirt, trousers, no shoes or socks, drinking
coffee from a cup.*

JIM *walks over to join them, sits in the spare chair. For
some time they listen to the music.*

JAMES. This is the *Agnus Dei*, I'll have to be going soon.
There's only the *Lux Eterna* to come.

KATE. How long does it take her from the Albert Hall?

JAMES. She gets a lift with one of the contraltos. A slow and
careful driver who likes to hang about chatting afterwards.

KATE. You're all right then.

JAMES. But not for long.

Sits on the settee. In moving to make room, KATE *lets her
gown slip and* JAMES *caresses her legs. Then he kisses her.
Then he resumes drinking.*

She turns down the volume.

KATE. Time to help yourself to another drop. It's simmering.

JIM. What does she want?

JAMES. No, really.

JIM. Not just me, surely?

KATE. You said you like the way I make it. Hot and strong.
Well, now you know where to find it. If you want it.

JIM. You've had the list of names. The introductions.

KATE. I hope you think it was worth waiting for.

JAMES. Absolutely.

JIM. Well –

JAMES. I'm surprised you need to ask.

JIM. But since you did, it wasn't, no.

JAMES. And thank you –

JIM. Wasn't worth the lying and fear and risk of discovery, no.

KATE. Thank *you*. It's been quite a while for me.

JIM. Pull the other. It's got bells on.

KATE. I went a bit mad after Albert's death but I've calmed down since.

JAMES. Did anyone stay the night of the funeral?

KATE. I'm not giving names.

JIM. So someone did.

JAMES. I wasn't asking.

KATE. I told you I wore that dress for you. I wanted you so much I nearly creamed myself. I couldn't face bed alone that night. But I have been behaving myself for nearly a month now. Which is why I was quick to come.

JAMES. I was afraid you found me slow.

KATE. Slow's best. Though quick's good too sometimes. Exciting and flattering.

JAMES. You didn't wear any scent.

KATE. No.

JAMES. Thoughtful.

JIM. I missed that scent.

JAMES. Nor any underclothes.

KATE. I know you like the wholesome approach.

JAMES. Who told you that?

KATE. Eleanor.

JIM. Christ.

KATE. I did my homework.

JAMES. You and Eleanor discussed underwear?

KATE. Women do, you know.

JIM. I didn't know.

KATE. We went shopping and I was buying the sort of lingerie Albert liked – black lacy satin knickers, suspenders, and she said you hated all that.

JIM. On her, yes.

JAMES. I thought Albert did as well.

KATE. Is that what he said?

JAMES. I assumed it. Men don't discuss underwear.

KATE. Oh, yes, he loved all that. When we first met he bought me several sets. He found it very arousing, specially in the shop.

JIM. Dirty bugger.

KATE. He couldn't resist me in the changing cubicle. With all the assistants outside, we had it standing up.

JIM. There isn't anything she wouldn't do.

KATE. Reflected in several mirrors.

JAMES. Talk about a dark horse.

JIM. He liked all that because your body's not attractive enough without.

KATE. He liked me to reek of scent.

JIM. That's the point, dear.

JAMES. I thought I knew him well.

JIM. Without the knocking-shop accoutrements, you're far from irresistible.

JAMES. I always thought him puritanical.

KATE. No way. I was never exclusively his. If I fancied someone else – or if he did –

JIM. You're out of your depth here, go!

KATE. You didn't think we were totally loyal?

JAMES (*shrugs*). I am.

KATE. No!

JAMES. Tonight's the first time.

KATE. Honestly?

JIM. And the last.

KATE. I'm very flattered.

JIM. Tell her it's the last time.

JAMES. Twenty-five years.

KATE. Staggering.

JAMES. Why? Millions live like that.

KATE. I've never thought of you as one of millions – owning and being owned. As I said, I hate ownership.

JAMES. It hasn't been like that.

KATE. No? Then what was to stop you?

JIM. Love, affection.

KATE. You can't have lacked opportunities.

JIM. Habit.

JAMES. Almost totally, I'd say.

JIM. Cowardice.

JAMES. Picture my life.

JIM. The fear of failure.

JAMES. My respectable working life. I walk fifteen yards through the kitchen, from the back door, across the garden to the workshop. Few excuses to go outside. Now and then I've felt the need but I've suppressed it, sublimated it –

KATE. Taken yourself in hand?

Pause. JIM *laughs, then* JAMES.

JAMES. It wasn't difficult. I've enjoyed my work, the pleasure of my craft. You could say it was more a vocation than a craft. More like being an original creative artist.

KATE. Right.

JIM. This is shit. You're a second-rater.

JAMES. To work on a Matisse or a Picasso means I play my humble part in keeping the wolves at bay. Lighting the darkness.

JIM. She'll never swallow that? She must be bursting.

JAMES. Well, that's my life. Eleanor knows what I'm doing every hour of the day.

JIM. Till now.

KATE. Oh, God, why's life never simple? Why another married man?

JIM. You tell me. Will you?

KATE. The last thing I want is to mess with marriages.

JIM. No. You won't. So non-committal.

KATE. And Eleanor of all people!

JIM. A mystery. Like all the young.

KATE. Such a fantastic woman.

JAMES. By Christ, isn't she? Outspoken, tolerant, realistic. Sensual.

KATE. We're very much alike in that way.

JIM. You're not sensual. Just pretending.

JAMES. Wonderfully sane as well.

JIM. Those words you used when you were coming. That wasn't sensuality. That was to help me, wasn't it?

KATE. So unlike Agnes in every way.

JIM. It's so good, you said.

JAMES. She can't stand Agnes.

JIM. Christ, you said, don't stop now, please . . .

JAMES. All bitter and twisted.

JIM. Or did I *really* excite you?

KATE. Thanks for warning me, by the way.

JIM. Come on, man.

KATE. About Agnes.

JAMES. The Requiem's finished. I must go, dear.

KATE. Come and stir my cup again soon.

She and JAMES *kiss.* JIM *watches and feels.*

JIM. Far less alarming the tongue, now it's not in public. Also
she smokes too much. Thank God it wasn't very good. It's
better with Eleanor. Thank Christ. And what's more to the
point, thank *you* for reminding me that I'm naturally
monogamous. I love my wife. So let's go home. Come on,
man, it's up to you to finish. Now and forever.

JAMES. It might be as well if you came to dinner. Then I can
give you those names I gave you at lunch.

KATE. And I can invite you to my private view.

JAMES. Absolutely.

KATE. I'll ring her and fix it.

They leave her and her room moves off.

JIM (*comes downstage and speaks to* JAMES). Home well
before her and no suspicion. She was so full of the concert
and how badly the soloist had sung the Recordare. Entirely
trusting.

JAMES. I was aching to tell her where I'd been.

JIM. We'd always said we would.

JAMES. The fact remains I didn't. As it was a solitary episode,
over as soon as started, I thought it was best forgotten.

JIM. So you'd enjoyed the broadcast –

JAMES. Nobody had telephoned –

JIM. Which I knew from the answering machine –

JAMES. And my love for the woman who shared my life was soon a tremendous physical desire. She's still the best looking even though she's old.

JIM. That night and the next few days you were never off the nest.

JAMES. We hadn't made love like that for years.

JIM. Then Kate invited herself to dinner and both of us trod a minefield of lies all evening trying to remember what Eleanor was supposed to know and not to know.

JAMES. I kept on yawning till she went.

They have brought on glasses and ELEANOR *opens the hall door and comes in.*

ELEANOR (*calls off*). Bye-bye, Kate. See you Tuesday. At the gallery! (*She closes the door*).

JAMES waits for her to return to the living room. As she enters, he yawns.

JAMES. Quarter past twelve. A slight improvement.

ELEANOR *doesn't answer but bustles about clearing up.*

I've done the ashtray. Ten cigarette-ends.

JIM. Why doesn't she answer?

JAMES. You must admit I'm right. She *is* a pale imitation of Albert.

Pause. ELEANOR *collects glasses.*

JIM (*urgently, to* JAMES). Has she got there? Christ!

JAMES. Well, we've done our duty for another month.

ELEANOR. Not quite.

She leaves the room for the hall, taking the glasses out.

JAMES. What d'you mean?

JIM. She means Kate's invited us to her –

ELEANOR. She's invited us to her Private View. (*She goes off to the kitchen*).

JAMES. Her Private View of what?

JIM. If she's even slightly suspicious, say you'd rather not go.

ELEANOR (*returning*). What d'you think?

JAMES. Well, photographs, presumably. Isn't that what she is, a photographer?

ELEANOR. Her photographs of the Far East, yes, taken when she and Albert were there together.

JAMES. Oh, no!

ELEANOR. Oh, yes! She asked me in the kitchen.

JAMES. Why didn't she ask us both together?

ELEANOR. She was afraid you'd say 'Oh, no', that's why. Afraid you'd bite her head off.

JIM. She's nowhere near!

JAMES. Me?

ELEANOR. You have been all the evening.

JAMES. *I* have?

ELEANOR. Ever since Albert's death, in fact.

JAMES. I wasn't aware of it.

ELEANOR. You're not a very aware person.

JIM (*sympathetically*). Oh, my darling!

ELEANOR. – or else you'd see your good opinion means a lot to her.

He has bolted the front door. She has put out the living room lights.

JIM (*to* JAMES). Like taking sweets from a baby.

ELEANOR. And yet when you're not biting her head off, you're yawning and looking at your watch.

JAMES. I sent her that list of names and addresses in the Middle East.

ELEANOR. She told me. But I should have thought you might have taken her out –

JIM. Taken her out?

ELEANOR. – and described all the people and how to approach them –

JAMES. Taken her out?

ELEANOR. Yes, to lunch.

JAMES. To lunch?

JIM. You should have told her.

ELEANOR. She sees you as a sort of irascible uncle figure who has to be appeased.

JAMES. How d'you know?

ELEANOR. What?

JAMES. How d'you know she doesn't see me as a very attractive man?

JIM. Careful!

JAMES. She *said* she did.

ELEANOR. She probably does because you are. But as she can't expect any change in that department is it too much to ask you to go and see her Private View?

JAMES. Too much by far. All up to the West End to drink Algerian Burgundy while a gang of buffers shout at me through a cloud of tobacco smoke and you know my view of photography, give a chimpanzee camera for a few hours.

They have climbed the stairs and she turns at the bedroom door, angrily.

ELEANOR. It wouldn't hurt you to do something generous for once! An act that didn't, in some way, contribute to your own selfish pleasure! (*She goes into the bedroom.*)

JAMES (*following*). All right, all right, have it your own way. We'll go. (*He slams the door behind him.*)

JIM rushes up the stairs.

JIM. Brilliant! Bravo!

A burst of joyful singing from the Ode in Beethoven's Ninth.

The entire Company comes on, moving screens to reveal KATE's blown-up photographs: Japanese and Chinese faces, city scenes, temples, squalor. They are clearly GUESTS at the Private View, drinking, smoking, talking and laughing forcibly. KATE, wearing a plain, black cocktail dress moves across exchanging words, embracing GUESTS. At the same entrance she greets ELEANOR and JAMES who are just arriving. JIM has moved across from the bedroom door and follows KATE; he watches as they greet one another. KATE hands them glasses of red wine from a WAITER's tray.

The music ends. Now we hear the more subdued buzz of party talk.

KATE. Great to see you.

ELEANOR. We said we'd come.

KATE. Great. Really.

ELEANOR. I see a few familiar faces.

JAMES. Several important critics.

KATE. Right.

ELEANOR. Are they the ones with pubic hair on their chins?

JAMES. Absolutely.

ELEANOR. That's the only way I remember.

She and JAMES laugh.

JIM (*to KATE*). This is not the kind of Private View I want of you. For example, I'd rather see that dress in a heap on the floor.

KATE *leads* ELEANOR *and* JAMES *to meet other*
GUESTS *and leaves them talking while she meets others.*
JIM *stays with her as she drifts away.*

Or hanging on a door the way it was yesterday afternoon.
And you in that underwear! Are you wearing it now? And
that was astounding the other night in our house, with
Eleanor in the next room dealing with a music student – forgotten already? Shall I say it then, in front of all these people?

Turns to them all.

She took my hand and placed it high on her thigh, raising
her skirt and slightly opening her legs. She wasn't wearing
anything above the stockings except the belt. And all the
time we kept talking in loud voices about Cartier-Bresson
and was photography an art, and sotto voce I told you how
the nakedness excited me.

JAMES *is concentrating on his group but is in a good
position to look across at* KATE. *She greets another* MAN,
kissing him on the mouth.

Hullo, is he getting the tongue?

The kiss ends. JIM *shouts across to* JAMES.

No, not time enough!

No one, of course, takes any notice.

But has he got the look of someone who has already had it?
Have *all* these men? When they talk to her, their faces get
so mawkish.

(*To one of the* MEN). You can't possibly think that's
attractive? That alcoholic simper?

KATE *moves to another and* JIM *follows and speaks to him.*

That superior scowl . . . Do I do that? How can women find
men bearable? But obviously they *do. She* does.

The MAN *puts his arm round* KATE.

How d'you find the thought they've been there? Above the
stockings? Every one of them? I welcome it. I savour it.

Reminds me how unimportant the whole thing is. Either or both of us could finish it whenever we liked and the other wouldn't care. But then again, what *is* essential? Man can't live by bread alone and once you've tasted honey . . .

JAMES *and* ELEANOR *move to look at the exhibits.* JIM *goes with* KATE *to another group and points to* JAMES.

Look at me. I'm over here with my wife, ostensibly studying your snaps but actually begging you to look in my direction and speak to me with your eyes.

KATE *laughs with some* GUESTS.

Yes, me, the well-known husband! Please!

ELEANOR *has left* JAMES, *goes to* KATE.

You looked! Our eyes met. I made you, with the force of my lust for you.

After a word or two, ELEANOR *leads* KATE *back to* JAMES. *They discuss one of the photographs.*

Thanks, my dear, for fetching the girl I sleep with. So that she can promise with her eyes to be there next time I telephone and prepare herself (*To* KATE.) like you did yesterday – by washing away all trace of perfume, dressing in black stockings and suspenders – (*Then to* ELEANOR.) – yes, I know I didn't, but people *change*, that's what it's all about – *change* – (*And to* KATE *again.*) – and you'll wait on the bed you and Albert used to share while on the radio Eleanor and a hundred other choristers sing the *Ode to Joy*.

Again the music bursts out. The exhibition disappears as swiftly as possible by the GUESTS *turning the screen as they go out.*

JAMES *and* JIM *come forward and down and occupy the phone booth.* JAMES *takes coins from his pocket, sets them on the box in a pile, dials.*

KATE *enters by the door of her room as lights go up there. She's dressed as before, makes straight for the phone and lifts the receiver.*

The music ends.

KATE. Yes?

The pay tone is heard till JAMES feeds in coins.

JAMES. James here. James Croxley. Hullo?

KATE. How are you?

JAMES. All the better for hearing you.

KATE. It's been ages.

JAMES. It *seems* ages. It's only two weeks. How've you been?

KATE. I've been pretty busy. Which is good.

JAMES. Good. That's good. When am I going to see you again?

KATE (*shrugs*). Name the day.

JAMES. It's not that easy. Eleanor's hardly ever out. Once or twice I rang from home while she was shopping but you weren't there.

KATE. Most days I'm out.

JAMES. I can sometimes get away to shop for turps or framing. Evenings are tricky. I've come for a jog on the Common but the first three phones had been vandalised. When can I see you?

KATE. Tonight's no good.

JAMES. No, not tonight.

JIM. What's she doing tonight, I wonder?

JAMES. But how about next Monday? Eleanor's rehearsing, the first time for weeks.

KATE. Oh, bloody hell, I can't.

JAMES. Never mind.

JIM. First jealousy. Then relief. Let off the hook.

KATE. I'm sorry. I really am.

JIM. No danger Monday.

JAMES. Two weeks is too long.

JIM. You can get your breath back.

KATE. Two weeks too long.

JIM. Your heart can slow down again.

JAMES. There's so much I want to say to you.

JIM. You can go back to sleep.

JAMES. But not on the phone. And anyway this has been a marathon jog.

KATE. Why don't you write?

JAMES. Write?

JIM. Better not.

KATE. If I can't see you.

JIM. There'd be proof. She could show people –

JAMES. I don't know.

JIM. Eleanor, for instance –

KATE. Darling –

JIM. But why should she show people?

KATE. Don't you trust me?

JAMES (*as* JIM *puts hand on mouth*). Of course I do. I'll write.

JIM (*breaking away*). Dear Kate –

KATE. Of course, you won't get any answer –

JAMES. No, of course not –

JIM. Dearest Kate –

KATE. Except I could reply to *both* of you with secret messages for *you* to find . . .

JIM. My darling –

KATE. Art postcards. Classical tits and arse.

JAMES. Be careful . . .

> KATE *laughs and lights go on her. She goes.*

> JAMES *comes to join* JIM, *writing the letter.*

JIM. Darling Kate, I suddenly realised this is the first love letter I've written for twenty-five years. So try to overlook the stilted phraseology.

JAMES (*to* JIM). Is it a good idea to mention that? Does it make me unattractive?

JIM (*to* JAMES). No. Anyway this isn't a love letter, is it? That's why I'm so grateful. Love's got nothing to do with it. We ask nothing of each other except the occasional hour together and the pleasure of our bodies.

> *Lights up on tearoom, similar to restaurant,* ELEANOR *and* AGNES *enter and take the free table.* WAITRESS *comes to take their order.*

JAMES (*to* JIM). I wish it could be longer though. How can it be as good as with Eleanor when there's so little time to practise?

JIM (*writing*). I can't imagine why a nice young girl –

JAMES (*to* JIM). – a lovely girl –

JIM (*writing*). Why a *fantastic* girl like you should offer herself without strings to an old man –

JAMES (*to* JIM). An older man –

JIM (*writing*). To a man like me.

JAMES (*musing*). It's the kind of thing men want and women loathe, they always say.

JIM (*writing*). But whatever the reason, thanks.

> *The* WAITRESS *leaves the table,* ELEANOR *and* AGNES *talk.*

Because what you've brought me is not only marvellous fun but pure. Unadulterated.

AGNES. Oh, yes, I'm much better, thanks. My new work's exhausting but well worth while. We're really making progress towards a better deal for battered wives.

ELEANOR. High time.

AGNES. And as a battered wife myself, I feel –

ELEANOR (*laughing*). Oh, come on –

AGNES. No, I mean, it's partly a sublimation for my battered feelings but that's neither here nor there as long as I do some good. All do-gooders want to do themselves a bit of good as well.

ELEANOR. Absolutely.

WAITRESS *brings their tray.*

JIM (*to* JAMES). Whereas, of course, marriage is anything but pure.

JAMES. It's ownership and children and duty and illness –

JIM. And joint accounts and property –

JAMES. And being an open book –

JIM. But I won't go into that –

JAMES. Heavy scene, man.

They laugh as ELEANOR *pours tea.*

ELEANOR. I'm so relieved you're better. Tell the truth, I felt you were dwelling morbidly on Albert's memory.

AGNES (*taking tea*). Did you?

ELEANOR. You were so vindictive to Kate.

AGNES. You think so?

ELEANOR. And there was no way you could hurt her, so you'd be the one to suffer.

AGNES. Oh?

JIM (*to letter*). So not to get into that whole heavy scene –

JAMES. Yes, she'll like that –

JIM. - let me simply say I feel no guilt about having *you,* only a little in deceiving *her.*

AGNES. You underestimate me. We can make her suffer too.

ELEANOR. We?

AGNES. Oh, the children are with me. Some time ago, as part of a slimy attempt to win Susie over to his side, Albert gave her a key to his flat. The one where whatshername's still living. We've been using it to get in there and make an inventory of the contents.

ELEANOR. Oh, Agnes, no.

AGNES. Oh, Eleanor, yes. From the Oriental rugs to the Irish tea towels.

ELEANOR. Agnes, I'm very fond of you, I can't let you destroy your own peace of mind like this.

AGNES. Peace of mind is ignorance.

ELEANOR. You know that isn't true.

AGNES. Oh, I've learnt it is. The only real peace of mind comes from punishing evil.

ELEANOR. She's not evil, she's a good-time girl.

AGNES. A star-fucker? That's what I thought. All the same, she destroyed my marriage.

ELEANOR. There must have been something wrong already. With your marriage.

JIM. So few things in life are pure and harmless.

JAMES. This must be. There's nothing else in it for her. Pure. Unadulterated.

ELEANOR. I'm sorry that sounds unkind but if old friends can't be helpful, who can?

AGNES. What should we do without old friends?

ELEANOR. Why don't we talk about something else? It obviously upsets you –

AGNES. Oh, no, one good turn deserves another. I'd like to help *you* too.

JIM has taken an official-looking envelope and writes an address. JAMES has got out a dictionary and is looking up a word.

JAMES. Adult, adulter, adulterate –

AGNES. When Susie was in the flat one day, the star-fucker being fucked in Sweden at the time, the mail came bumping through the front door onto the welcome mat.

JAMES. Adulterate. 'To render corrupt, by base admixture.'

JIM (*to* JAMES). The opposite of pure.

He puts a stamp on the envelope. AGNES *opens her bag and takes out an exactly similar envelope.*

AGNES. She opened all the official-looking letters to see if there was something we should be sharing.

ELEANOR. Honestly, Agnes, reading people's mail!

JAMES. Adultery. 'Violation of the marriage bed. Image-worship.'

AGNES. And as it turned out, there was.

JIM (*to* JAMES). Really? Image-worship?

JAMES. 'Enjoyment of a benefice during the translation of a bishop.'

He and JIM *laugh.*

JIM. Trust the bloody clergy to get it wrong.

He scans the last part of the letter as JAMES *puts away the dictionary.*

ELEANOR *does not immediately take the letter but looks at it.*

AGNES. You'll recognise the handwriting?

JAMES. The dictionary's useless.

ELEANOR takes the letter.

What's pure *is* impure. Adulteration can clarify.

JIM. Purify.

During a pause, the sounds of the tearoom swell briefly while ELEANOR reads and AGNES sips her tea.

NELL dressed like ELEANOR, stands at the next table, where she's been sitting on her own with her back turned. She is between the two women.

NELL. 'Of course I'm longing to be in your bed again but there aren't many chances to leave the house. Later this year there's the Matthew Passion and towards Christmas the Mozart Requiem and Messiah. Some – or all – of these I hope we shall be listening to together.'

JAMES. With half an ear.

JIM (*writing*). With – half – an – ear.

Reading again.

NELL. If I can come at a time you haven't any other callers, though I understand I have no claims on you. Any more than you on me. Which strikes me as a perfect arrangement. And sometimes when you come round here, we'll feel each other up while Eleanor's in the music room. I like the way you whisper all that filth. And I liked it when you spilt wine from your mouth into mine. So – till the next rehearsal of a Passion, here's thinking of you, love, – all manner of kisses . . .

ELEANOR folds the letter and returns it to AGNES. JIM folds it too and the two letters are returned to the envelopes together. JIM seals his.

AGNES. Join the club. I've poured some tea.

ELEANOR. Thank you.

AGNES. I never meant to show you that.

NELL. Hah!

ELEANOR. I'm glad you did.

AGNES. Glad?

NELL. How could he do this to me?

ELEANOR. Glad, certainly, you didn't keep it to yourself, as it obviously troubled you so much.

NELL. How could he risk humiliating me?

AGNES. Doesn't it trouble *you*?

NELL. In front of her?

ELEANOR sips her tea.

ELEANOR. It troubles me you and Susie have read this letter. Has anyone else?

AGNES. Of course not.

NELL. My cheeks are burning.

AGNES. D'you want to keep it?

NELL. She's bound to notice.

ELEANOR. That might be best.

NELL. My world's caved in but I'm sitting here.

Taking the letter.

ELEANOR. Thanks.

NELL. Come on, get away as quick as you –

AGNES. Eleanor love, I only wanted to put you on your guard by a couple of subtle hints – but when you started *defending* her and saying she was harmless, I knew it was time to show you the letter.

NELL. Come on, you're enjoying every minute.

ELEANOR. I didn't call her 'harmless'. I said she wasn't evil, that's all, I think the letter proves it. And, of course, I knew she fancied James. In fact, I told him.

NELL. That much is true, make do with that.

AGNES. But did you know he listened to your concerts in the bed she used to share with Albert?

NELL. Try not to imagine it.

ELEANOR. He wants a bit on the side, why not?

She shrugs and smiles, drinks tea.

AGNES. That's what Albert called it too.

NELL. Make your mind a blank.

AGNES. His very words.

NELL. She pities you.

AGNES. A bit on the side. 'It's nothing', he said when I found out, 'she's nothing to me'.

NELL. Think of nothing or you'll cry.

AGNES. Be more tolerant, he used to say. More easy-going. He stood for tolerance. The permissive society. He did as much as anyone to advertise its virtues.

NELL. Why write a letter? Why take that risk?

AGNES. Well, now we see what that's led to – abortion, violence, the kids on drugs, apathy on one side and a neo-fascist law-and-order reaction on the other.

NELL. Shut up!

AGNES. It's not the first time liberalism has failed us. We should know better. Stop it now.

NELL. Shut up, I said!

AGNES. Don't try appeasement. You'll end at your own little Munich.

NELL (*to* ELEANOR). Come on.

JAMES *starts to use the phone.*

ELEANOR. Shan't be a minute, Agnes . . .

AGNES. Shall I come with you?

NELL. Haven't you had enough?

ELEANOR *goes, colliding with the* WAITRESS.

The dissonant fanfare from the Choral Symphony.

During this, the lights fade from the teashop as AGNES
beckons to the WAITRESS *who brings the bill. She pays
and goes.*

At the same time, JAMES *is joined in the living room by*
JIM. *Lights up on* KATE'*s room show that they are talking
on the phone. She has a bottle of scent in the other hand.*

The music ends.

KATE. Well, it certainly hasn't arrived.

JAMES. I hope to God it doesn't come back here.

KATE. The last few weeks a lot of my mail's gone missing.
Personal *and* official. Luckily my *work's* arranged by
phone.

JIM. Personal? That means from men.

JAMES. God save us from the Postal Service.

KATE (*laughing*). Right. Well, am I going to see you?

JIM. I wish she wouldn't say 'right' all the time.

JAMES. I can't today. She's expected back any minute.

KATE. No, not today. I've got to go out myself.

JIM (*into the receiver again*). Or some man's coming to have
you –

JAMES. Next Tuesday afternoon I'm going to bid for the
Arabs at Sotheby's Post Impressionist sale. I could drop in
on you for an hour or so –

KATE. Why don't we meet there?

JIM. You might be seen.

KATE. I'd love to see you bidding. Spending all those petro-
dollars. Very sexy.

JAMES. Oh, it's not at all, believe me –

KATE. Then you could touch me up while I'm driving back
here. With my hands on the wheel I'd be at your mercy.

JIM. Right.

ELEANOR *enters by the front door.* JAMES *reacts.* JIM *runs to the door to see, signals back to* JAMES.

It's Eleanor.

JAMES. Right you are then.

KATE. And I've got some soap the same as yours at home, so I can put on perfume this time and you can shower afterwards –

JAMES. Absolutely.

KATE. So she'll never know.

JAMES. Thank you very much.

ELEANOR *listened for a moment and now hangs her coat. When she returns, it is with* NELL.

KATE. I'm not just a pretty face and a pair of tits, you know –

JAMES. Goodbye. (JAMES *puts down phone*).

NELL. Ting. D'you think that was her?

JIM *returns to* JAMES, *who stands listening.* KATE *looks at the phone, sprays her neck and ears with scent and leaves the room as lights go.*

JIM. That was Otto instructing you to buy Pissaros –

NELL. Is this what it's been then all the time?

JAMES (*going to meet her*). Hullo, love.

NELL. Is this what it's going to be like from now on?

JAMES. How are you?

NELL. So transparent! Christ, why did I never notice?

JAMES. How was your afternoon?

Tries to kiss ELEANOR *but she evades him and goes into living room.* JIM *and* NELL *go with them.*

JIM. What's this? What's up with her?

JAMES. I got on pretty well. The Douanier Rousseau's nearly finished. I ate my sandwiches – delicious by the way – and got to feeling rather lonely. Randy.

NELL. So rang her for a horny chat?

He goes to ELEANOR *and embraces her from behind. She pushes him off.*

And now you want me for a wank?

JIM. Something's up.

JAMES. How was Agnes?

NELL (*to him*). How would you expect?

JAMES. More easy-going? Or still 'hard-done-by'?

NELL. Bastard!

JAMES. Still the wronged woman?

NELL. Bastard sod!

JIM. Don't talk too much. You don't usually talk this much!

ELEANOR *moves about, hiding her face from him. She shrugs. Silence.*

NELL (*to* ELEANOR). Don't let it drift. You can't.

ELEANOR. Who were you on the phone to?

JAMES. Just now, you mean?

ELEANOR. As I came in.

JIM. Otto –

JAMES. Otto.

JIM. The Black Widow has told her something.

JAMES. Instructing me to buy Pissaros and Signacs at the sale on Tuesday.

NELL. You can't lie to save your life.

JAMES. The sheikhs are interested, so those particular painters must have gone up a few points.

NELL (*over part of this*). Wouldn't deceive a cretin surely?

JIM (*as* ELEANOR *turns*). She's been crying.

NELL. He deceived *you.*

JAMES. Can I get you a drink?

NELL. A trusting wife must be easier than a cretin.

JAMES. Vodka and tonic?

ELEANOR's taken the letter out and hands it to him.

ELEANOR. Returned to sender.

He takes it and looks at it. She gets herself a drink.

JAMES. How d'you get this?

NELL. Does it matter?

JIM. Saint Agnes.

NELL. Not from Kate if that's what you're thinking.

JAMES. Kate told me it hadn't arrived.

NELL. When you last went to fuck her? Or on the phone as I came in?

JAMES. She was on the phone as you came in.

JIM. Truth time. Good!

JAMES. I shouldn't have written it, but now it's out, I'm glad. You're the only one I wanted to tell and the only one I couldn't.

ELEANOR. You wanted to tell *me*? Tell me you were screwing a girl who's younger than our daughter?

JAMES. We always said we'd tell each other if and when –

ELEANOR. *You* did. My way was to keep it dark.

NELL. Which I did.

JAMES. Funny how things turn out.

ELEANOR. What?

JAMES. In the event, I've told the lies and you've been straight.

ELEANOR. You can't be serious.

NELL. Go on, tell him. Wipe that self-satisfied look off his face –

JAMES. What's that mean?

NELL. That I've been a naughty boy but ain't I clever expression right off his –

ELEANOR. Nothing.

JAMES. I've lied to you and I'm sorry.

ELEANOR. How long have you been shagging Kate?

JIM (*insulted*). Shagging?

JAMES. I've been meeting her for a few weeks.

ELEANOR. A few weeks and I know already! God, you couldn't fool a cretin.

JAMES. My heart wasn't in it really.

NELL. Tell him how long you lied to *him*. How long you spared *his* feelings. Go on!

JAMES. As I said, I wanted to tell you. I'm glad you know.

NELL. I didn't want to know.

JAMES. I've always been very proud of the way we trusted each other. I totally trusted you and knew you'd have told me if any other man –

ELEANOR. No, no, that wasn't what *I* agreed. I said if it happened, spare the other's feelings.

NELL. As I did yours.

ELEANOR. Keep it dark.

JIM. She's cracked.

JAMES. I understood the opposite. If you'd had a lover, you'd have told me.

NELL. You'd have been destroyed.

ELEANOR. I certainly would not have told you. You loved me then.

JAMES. I love you now.

NELL. I've read that letter! Four times. Once at the table of the teashop in front of the friend who gave it to me. Twice in the lavatory, once more in the train home. You called her 'darling'.

ELEANOR *shakes her head and goes for another drink.*

JAMES. Who gave you this? Saint Agnes?

NELL. How could you humiliate me in front of her?

JIM. Who else could it be?

NELL. Don't you see that's the worst of it? The loss of dignity.

JAMES. She's an interfering bitch.

ELEANOR. She's a poor widow possessed by love.

JIM. Don't keep using that word.

JAMES. Love? She wanted to hurt you.

NELL. Who gave her the opportunity?

JIM. I must warn Kate.

ELEANOR. I thought that at first. And for some moments I considered hurting Agnes in return.

JAMES. *How* could you have hurt her?

NELL. Go on, tell him.

She waits. ELEANOR *doesn't speak. To him, decisively.*

She still thinks –

ELEANOR. She still thinks Albert only had *one* other woman. The one you've taken over.

JAMES. I haven't taken her –

ELEANOR. Whereas I know of at least one other.

JAMES. Kate told me there were others, yes.

ELEANOR. This was before Kate.

JAMES. How d'you know?

NELL. He's hooked. Go on.

JAMES. You can't be sure.

ELEANOR. I know the only way you *can* be sure.

She sits and drinks. NELL *studies* JAMES.

NELL. Are you getting there? How long can it possibly take –

JIM. Her?

JAMES. D'you mean – ?

JIM. Christ!

JAMES. You and Albert?

NELL. Talk about the Mills of God.

ELEANOR. Yes.

JAMES. Really?

NELL. Really, yes.

JIM. You never know anyone.

JAMES. When was this?

ELEANOR. In another century.

JAMES. Where? For how long?

NELL. How does it feel? Eh?

ELEANOR. I'm not going into details now –

JIM. Oh, yes you are –

ELEANOR. – because it wasn't important.

NELL. Even *that's* hurt him. Don't go further. Leave it there.

ELEANOR. An episode. A shoulder to cry on. After a few
    drinks. You were away.

JAMES. Where did you –– ?

ELEANOR. Here. He brought me home.

JAMES. In our bed?

ELEANOR. In this room. Once. Nothing more.

   JAMES *recoils from the sofa then turns away to get a drink.*

JAMES. Was it all right?

ELEANOR. I'm not going into details.

JIM *goes to* JAMES *and talks inaudibly.*

NELL. That's enough. He's had enough. Don't lose your advantage by saying it was hopeless, that you both felt ashamed of betraying James. Violating the taboo of best friends' wives or husbands. Leave it at that.

JAMES *turns back smiling. They chuckle together.*

JAMES. I must say, he had some sauce.

JIM. In this room, eh?

JAMES. Crafty bugger.

NELL. He's smiling. He admires him even more.

JAMES. I always thought he was true to Agnes till he went for Kate. But now it seems he poked everything in sight. Including you.

JIM (*to heaven*). Well, can you hear me? You've had my wife. I've had your girl. Still am having her. Knock for knock.

JAMES. Tit for tat.

He and JIM *chuckle together.*

NELL. Christ, the camaraderie of cock. How they literally stand together! Whereas women never trust each other.

ELEANOR. You think it's funny?

NELL. Agnes can't trust me, I can't trust Kate –

JAMES. That you had Albert? Not that funny, no.

NELL. Though of course James can't trust *you* now. Perhaps his smile was only a bluff. He must feel hurt –

ELEANOR. The episode with Albert was more mess that ecstasy. A quick bang after a party with the kids asleep upstairs and Sarah Vaughan on the hi-fi. Not important.

JAMES. Like me and Kate.

NELL. But unlike the man I nearly left you for.

ELEANOR. If it's unimportant, why write a letter?

JIM (*to* JAMES). Exactly. What the hell did you write for?

NELL (*to* JAMES). Two years I had a sort of love affair and I never wrote a letter!

JAMES. I don't know.

NELL. Yes, he was in the choir. That's how we could meet once or twice a week without your finding out.

JAMES. So many years since I wrote that sort of letter. I wanted to see if I could remember how . . .

ELEANOR. You never wrote *me* that sort of letter.

NELL (*to* ELEANOR). Don't tell him, though. He'd discount it because you never went to bed.

ELEANOR. If it's as unimportant as you say, you won't mind giving her up?

NELL. He'd call it romantic.

JAMES. Of course not.

JIM (*warning*). Steady!

NELL. I had the best of both worlds – him for flattery, you for bed and breakfast.

ELEANOR. So!

JAMES. So!

NELL. So you see I'm not a stranger in this house. Very much at home, in fact.

ELEANOR. There's not going to be any in-between. Either you go with her or stay with me.

JIM (*to* JAMES). Agree to anything.

JAMES. I never intended going anywhere with her. And she wouldn't want me to.

ELEANOR. Don't be simple, James.

NELL. It was your simplicity made me stay. I couldn't see how you'd manage without me.

JAMES. She doesn't want another married scene.

ELEANOR. She was after Albert and she's after you.

JIM (*excited*). D'you think that's possible?

JAMES. Absolutely not.

NELL. You'll be telling us next this is only a bit on the –

JAMES. Eleanor, for both of us this is only a bit on the side.

ELEANOR. Oh! (*Howling.*)

NELL. No!

JAMES (*angry*). What?

ELEANOR. That's what they *all* say. That's what Albert told Agnes.

NELL. About the same girl.

JIM (*to* ELEANOR). Can't you see this is doing us good?

ELEANOR. Perhaps she's funny for old men, loves her father, hates her mother, wants to hurt all women, I don't know.

JIM. This is enlarging us!

ELEANOR. Albert at least was celebrated. A star to fuck.

JAMES. You haven't stopped using off-colour language since you came in.

JIM. Fuck and bang and shagging and love.

JAMES. Albert's marriage was on its last legs. Ours is different. You're not Agnes.

JIM. So don't act like her.

JAMES. She treated Albert as property. But people aren't things.

ELEANOR. So nor is Kate. Not a bit on the side but a woman.

NELL. Both.

ELEANOR. She wants to take you away from me. I know her. I was like her once. Well, go with her if that's what you want.

NELL. And if you do, where does that leave *me*. A man of fifty's still all right but a grandmother is nobody's idea of –

JAMES. There's no question of leaving you.

Choral music, perhaps 'Quam Olim Abrahae' from
Mozart's Requiem or a fugue from a Passion.

KATE *comes on wearing a gown and arrives downstage at*
the same time as JIM. *Lights change.* JIM *and* KATE *face*
front.

JIM. Hullo, Kate?

KATE. Hullo?

JIM. James speaking. James Croxley.

KATE. I know who it *is*. How *are* you?

JIM. Eleanor's found out.

KATE. Oh, no. How?

JIM. The letter I wrote got to her instead.

KATE. Through Agnes?

JIM. Yes.

KATE. I thought as much. They've got a key.

JIM. Of course I'll have to write an official letter.

KATE. Of course.

JIM. Ignore it.

KATE. Right.

JAMES *comes down too.*

KATE *continues to* JIM, *describing how she came to*
suspect AGNES *was prying. The rest of the Act works like*
this – a fugue of voices, the written speeches predominating
and improvised dialogue continued behind.

JAMES. Dear Kate, it doesn't matter how, but Eleanor's
discovered we've been meeting. I suppose it's only natural
she should be upset but I've tried to explain it was only a
lark and there's no question of anything more.

ELEANOR (*joining them, while* JAMES, KATE *and* JIM
continue). Dear Kate, I haven't read his letter but I hope
James didn't give the impression I'm getting melodramatic.

There's no need for any of us to get into a heavy scene, as
he calls it.

KATE. Dearest Eleanor, thank you so much for writing. The
worst thing about all this is the pain I've caused you –

NELL (*joining them*). Oh, yes. I'm sure –

KATE. – and the thought of losing your friendship.

NELL. You do seem to have your work cut out staying friendly
with the wives.

ELEANOR. I've told him he's at liberty to go with you but if
he does, it's for good. No using you as lover and me as
safety net.

NELL. You have him and the best of luck. Find out for
yourself what fun it is to be the wife of a man who works at
home.

JAMES. Eleanor and I both hope that, when this has spent
itself, we'll all three pick up the pieces again and meet as
friends . . .

NELL. No chance of a break or change of scene. Well, you've
given him that. So take him, do his washing, his VAT . . .

KATE. Let's please meet and talk as soon as I'm back from
foreign parts.

JIM. I know that while you're – where is it?

KATE. Kyoto, Tokyo, Nagasaki, Los Angeles, San Francisco –

JIM. Yes, I know you'll have every man who comes your way –

JAMES. Comes – your – way.

KATE. Is it enough to say at the moment that my affection and
respect for you have never diminished?

NELL. I'd rather be the mistress, with all the little mistressy
excitements: will he come today, will *she* find out? I might
suggest that – let him live with you and sneak away
whenever he can for a crafty fuck with me.

JIM. And, though I long to be in their place, I don't resent you
having those men. We don't love each other and you don't
love them –

NELL. And I'll dress in frilly undies and wear exotic scent and enjoy the aphrodisiac of fooling you, the wife.

JAMES. And if by chance Susie or Agnes is reading this, do let it through because it's written with Eleanor's approval and I've kept a carbon copy. (*To* ELEANOR). Let's go for a lie-down, shall we?

ELEANOR. Why not? Two hours before my student comes.

JIM. All I ask is, while you're having them, spare a thought for me. On similar occasions I'll remember you . . .

JAMES and ELEANOR *move to the stairs.*

KATE. I'm so brought down and confused by all the trouble I've caused . . .

JIM. By Christ, Kate, I'll miss you . . .

KATE. . . . you'll survive . . .

JIM. Just about.

KATE. Till I get back . . .

JAMES and ELEANOR *have climbed the stairs and near the top* JAMES *begins caressing her. She responds and they embrace on the top step.*

NELL. Listen to his fifty-year-old moans about his failing health . . . his wasted life, the girls he never had . . .

JIM. Send a sexy card –

KATE. All right –

JIM. With a hidden message for me.

NELL. But why should you take him from me? He's mine! I love him!

They all continue.

JAMES and ELEANOR *make love on the landing.*

Music drowns all voices.

ACT TWO

The Chorale 'O Haupt von Blut Und Wunden' from Bach's St Matthew's Passion.

After some time, the lights show ELEANOR *in the living room, a score on her knee, listening. Nearby is* NELL *trying to write a letter.*

In the workroom, JAMES *is restoring a Victorian head of Christ crucified.* JIM *near him reading a book.*

For a while this tableau is almost still. First ELEANOR *puts down her score and goes to refill her glass with vodka and tonic.*

JAMES *throws down his brush and wipes his hands on a rag.* JIM *looks up at him.* JAMES *studies the painting.*

ELEANOR *returns to the sofa, drinking.* NELL *crumples the page she's been writing, starts again.*

JIM *takes the painting off the easel and goes to the door with it.* JIM *follows.*

The kitchen door at once opens and they enter the living room. Neither of the women hear them. JAMES *stands listening to the music till the chorus ends with 'So shandlich Zugericht'. Recitative continues quietly.*

JAMES. What does all that mean?

ELEANOR (*startled*). Hullo.

NELL *hides the letter.*

JAMES. What's it all about?

ELEANOR (*translating*). Something like 'Head full of blood and wounds, full of sorrow and scoffing, mocked with a crown of thorns'.

JAMES. I thought so.

He goes to get himself a drink, putting down the painting against a chair.

NELL (*reads*). Dear James, it's funny writing a letter to someone you live with but there are things to say now that I suddenly find I can't say to your face.

JAMES. Want a drink?

ELEANOR. Won't say no.

She finishes the one she's got.

Vodka and tonic.

NELL. While Kate's been away these last few weeks, I've learnt that I don't hate her. If anything, I 'm grateful to her, for giving our marriage a shot in the arm.

ELEANOR. That's not right . . .

JAMES (*turning from drinks cabinet*). What?

ELEANOR (*waking, faking*). It can't be a diminuendo.

JAMES *gives her the drink.*

I'm marking my score of the Matthew Passion and getting quietly sloshed.

JAMES. Ah. Well, cheers.

ELEANOR. Finished the painting?

JAMES. I couldn't face any more without a Scotch. Had more than enough of that insipid eunuch. (*Shows her the picture.*) The self-pity. Sickly. Sentimental.

ELEANOR. You're getting very well paid, aren't you—?

JAMES. I asked more than I thought they'd give. And they said yes.

NELL. Thirty pieces of silver?

ELEANOR *laughs.*

JIM. It's not funny.

JAMES (*intensely*). We still live in the shadow of His death. And His birth for that matter. A virgin birth. A conception and a birth without carnal love. It flies in the face of all we know and people like us don't believe it any more – but two thousand years of history are sitting on our backs.

JIM (*to* JAMES). She doesn't know what you're saying. (*To* ELEANOR.) This is all about *us*. What's happening to you and me.

ELEANOR. The music's Christian and I like that.

JAMES. Of course. It's Bach. But what if it's this sickly Victoriana?

JIM. The holy oil that kept the wheels of industry turning?

JAMES. Propaganda for the satanic mills. Putting a love of God in place of love of people. (*To the picture.*) 'Thou hast conquered. Oh pale Galilean –'

JIM (*reading*). 'The world has grown grey from Thy breath – '

JAMES. Poor old Swinburne must have had a bellyful of sanctity.

JIM. No wonder he spent his last years being flogged by whores!

JAMES. Even a healthy sexual passion was twisted into a craving for the infinite. The anti-lifers, the troubadours, the saints and martyrs. Saint Teresa caught by Bernini mid-orgasm, pierced by the lance of God. Anyone who's ever watched their partner in the act can see that's a woman coming. But Bernini thought he was carving Saint Teresa, or said he did. By her account 'when he drew it out I thought my entrails would have been torn out too and when he left me I glowed in the hot fire of love for God'.

JIM *goes. Shows* ELEANOR *the book.*

NELL. He's worked himself into a lather, hasn't he? That usually means he's got some book.

ELEANOR. Have you been reading a book or what?

JIM (*resentfully*). Books are to help us understand.

JAMES. I do want to make some sense of my life, don't you?

ELEANOR. Of course.

JAMES. And not in terms of death.

NELL. He means her.

ELEANOR. Well, *we* don't see it like that, do we?

NELL. He means why can't he have *her* too?

ELEANOR. We're not Christians. I'm an atheist but I love church music and oratorio and hymns and Christmas carols. Hundreds of people singing together is the nearest we may ever come to heaven on earth. Communion.

JAMES. The Communion is a ceremony based on the pre-Christian orgy.

JIM. Dearest Kate, are you doing it now? At this moment are you saying to some other man what you said to me?

JAMES. The pagan fertility festivals? The Christians took them over.

ELEANOR. I meant 'communion' in the sense of people congregating.

JIM. Are you saying 'don't stop now, please' to some lucky Yank?

JAMES. People used to congregate to make love. Before the God-lovers and life-haters set down the couple as the largest legitimate sexual group.

ELEANOR. You've got sex in the head.

JIM. Where else can I have it?

NELL. She's in there, isn't she? In your head? With her frilly knickers and tricks with the wine?

ELEANOR. Has all this come from having a bit on the side?

JAMES. Either/or's not the answer. If it finishes with a new monogamy.

ELEANOR. It's hard to see an alternative.

JAMES. More than one.

ELEANOR. At a time?

JIM *and* NELL *listen.*

JAMES. Why not?

ELEANOR. It's hard enough to find one person you fancy, leave alone two.

NELL. It took you twenty-five years to find Kate.

ELEANOR. I mean, I'm game. But where do we look?

NELL. And *she's* in California, so –

ELEANOR. Shall we go through the phone book or what?

JIM. You'd better take this seriously.

JAMES (*laughing*). We could go round the pub, see who we run into.

NELL. Anyone fancy a fertility festival?

JAMES *and* ELEANOR *embrace.*

Good clean house. Cold buffet to follow. (*She closes her eyes.*) Oh, my love, stop doing that with your tongue.

Doorbell rings.

ELEANOR. That's my student. She wants me to run through her adjudication pieces. Sorry.

JAMES. Oh well. I'd better get back to Old Killjoy here.

ELEANOR *goes towards the door.* JAMES *takes the picture to the kitchen.* JIM *talks after* ELEANOR.

JIM. I won't allow my life to close in again. I got my chance and opened the door. If I can change, then so can you –

ELEANOR *opens the door to* KATE.

KATE. Hullo.

JIM. It's her. She's here!

ELEANOR. Good God!

KATE. Bad time?

ELEANOR. Not at all. Come in.

> KATE *does.* ELEANOR *shuts door.* JIM *runs back to* JAMES.

JIM. I made you come by thinking of you. By dwelling on your memory. Night and day.

KATE. You said to drop in if I was passing.

ELEANOR. Of course. Delighted.

NELL. Where would you be passing *to*?

ELEANOR. I thought you were still abroad.

KATE. Been back a few days.

> ELEANOR *takes* KATE's *outdoor coat and goes to hang it.*

JIM. A few days. Why d'you leave it a few days?

ELEANOR. You're looking well. Wonderful colour.

KATE. That's California.

NELL. And dressed to kill. Kill *what*?

KATE. Won't last long in London.

NELL. Cost the earth, that little number.

ELEANOR. James is here.

NELL. The same perfume I smelt on James that day. That he said was from expensive tarts and now I know what he meant.

> *They go into the living room.*

ELEANOR. We've got company.

JAMES (*turning, coming to greet* KATE). So I heard.

JIM. Kiss? No.

> KATE *and* JAMES *shake hands.*

KATE. Oh, very formal. Surely we're allowed a friendly kiss?

> *They do. A social peck.*

NELL. What's the game now? Can't be after him or she
wouldn't have come here. Or would she?

ELEANOR. Lovely tan, hasn't she James?

JAMES. Absolutely. As you told us in your card from – where
was it?

KATE. Santa Monica?

JIM. Saucy as ever. A nude by Ingres –

KATE. You got that then?

JIM. – with an arse like a peach –

JAMES. Yes, indeed.

JIM. – And a hope that both of us would see your tan before it
faded away.

KATE. I'm brown all over.

JIM. Or as you said 'the tail-end of your tan'.

KATE. For the first time ever.

JIM. Tail end!

JAMES. Can I get you a drink?

KATE. I thought you'd never ask.

JAMES. Gin and tonic?

KATE. Right.

NELL (*to* ELEANOR). Strange to watch the two of you
together. First time since I found out . . .

JAMES. And you, love? Same again?

ELEANOR. Mmmmm?

JAMES. Same again?

ELEANOR. Please.

NELL. Aren't you drinking rather a lot?

ELEANOR. I'm not driving.

JAMES. What?

JIM. What's she talking about?

NELL. You're pissed.

She moves off unsteadily.

JIM (*to* KATE). Find a way of saying if you got my letter.

JAMES. You had a good time, then?

KATE. Great, fantastic! In California anyway.

JIM. No, wait till the student comes.

ELEANOR. Get any work done?

KATE. In Japan I worked. In the States I played.

JIM. Then when Eleanor's in the music room you can say if it's yes to Zurich.

ELEANOR. Lucky girl.

NELL. Everything's instant isn't it? Casual. Spur of the moment.

JIM. You'll like it. Three days. Nice hotel. The lake, the mountains.

KATE. Lucky . . . in some ways.

NELL. Arrivals, departures, eating, drinking, who you sleep with.

ELEANOR. Some ways?

JIM. And while I'm working you can shop. I'm being paid in francs.

ELEANOR. Why 'some ways'?

NELL. She even makes her pictures with a shutter. Instantly.

ELEANOR. No strings and no connections.

JAMES has given drinks.

JAMES. Cheers, then.

KATE. Right.

NELL. I was like you once. At college. The fun-loving dolly.

JIM. I hoped you'd reply to my dealer – marking the envelope 'To be collected'.

KATE. So here we are again, all three of us. I've missed you both. I meant what I said in my letter. This thing James and I have had, we won't let that affect our relationship, will we?

ELEANOR. We're adult people.

NELL. What's she doing here – dressed to kill? What's her game?

KATE *takes* ELEANOR's *hand.*

KATE. If I'd been you I'd have scratched my eyes out.

ELEANOR. Really? No.

KATE. Yes, a very heavy scene. But it was only a 'lark'. Wasn't it, James?

JIM. I want you.

JAMES. I hope I've made that clear.

ELEANOR. He's tried.

KATE (*to* ELEANOR). I'd have felt far worse to lose *you.*

She kisses ELEANOR's *hand, then her lips.*

NELL. Is she lesbian, then?

JIM. This is either an elaborate cover or –

NELL. It would account for the string of married men.

ELEANOR. I felt the same about you.

NELL. Indirectly getting at the wives.

KATE. You may not believe this but I can't stand all that underhand business.

JIM. This is good but where's it leading?

KATE. I know you agree with me, Eleanor, that sex is terrific fun as long as it doesn't lose you friends. It should be open.

Cards on the table.

JIM and NELL talk to JAMES and ELEANOR but we don't hear clearly and KATE continues:

If I like the look of a man or another woman – or both – I ought to say so and see what happens. I mean, I shouldn't be put down by conventional values and start a lot of lying that nearly led to losing *both*.

She reaches for JAMES's hand and he approaches. She holds both.

I'm putting this very badly –

JIM. I wouldn't say that.

NELL. Oh, I don't know –

KATE. – but d'you know what I mean, James?

JAMES. Yes, I believe so.

JIM. Just taking your hand has given me a hard-on.

NELL. She wants us both.

KATE. I know Eleanor does.

JIM. She's come for a sandwich!

KATE. I don't mean I wasn't attracted to you, James, of course I was, but not you only. It was both of you. Your life. Your whole relationship. You know?

She kisses him as before.

JIM. You're doing beautifully.

NELL. I can feel his desire through her. I suppose that's how it works. A sort of conductor.

JAMES moves away. KATE breaks from ELEANOR, who sits.

ELEANOR. I'm sure he understands. I do.

JAMES. We were talking about this before you arrived.

JIM (*behind her*). We know what you mean, both of us.

He runs his hands up and down her body, caressing her.

KATE. Well, I realised how I felt about you both when it all came out and it was in that mood I left for Japan. I tried to keep my head by working hard while I was there but on my last night I was taking some pictures of an American diplomat and his Japanese wife who finally made it clear they'd like me to stay the night.

ELEANOR. And did you?

JIM *runs his hand up her leg, kneeling now beside her. He raises her skirt, showing her thigh.*

KATE. I did, yes.

JIM. Wear this dress when you come to bed. Let Eleanor take it off.

JAMES. Japanese women seem too – I don't know – too much like porcelain – for a night of hanky-panky.

KATE. It's when the porcelain cracks, though.

NELL. The thought of another woman never aroused me, but a man as well –

ELEANOR. You enjoyed it then?

NELL. *That* man –

KATE. No.

She goes to sit, leaving JIM. *But he follows and kneels by her, caressing her leg.* NELL *goes to* JAMES *and embraces him.*

JAMES. Why not?

NELL. Maybe this is the best solution. I'm fond of her and you desire her and I love you.

KATE. The man was only interested in stimulating *her.* I felt left out in the end. Aroused but unsatisfied –

NELL. But can I watch you have her?

ELEANOR. Perhaps somebody's always left out.

JIM (*embracing her*). You won't be left out. I want you both.

JAMES. But there was nothing wrong in principle?

KATE. Oh, no.

JAMES. Especially in a non-Christian country. Before the Holy Ghost started haunting us, sex in crowds was the norm. Romantic passion for one's beloved was to the Greeks and Romans an affliction you hoped wouldn't happen in your family.

KATE. I must say I've usually enjoyed it, Christian country or not. Another drink, James, please.

JAMES. And you, love?

ELEANOR. A little Dutch courage, yes.

JAMES *gets the drinks.*

NELL. Who begins and how?

KATE. Anyway. I left before either of them were up and hitched back into town on a truck, which was another unsatisfactory episode –

NELL. Are you making this up?

KATE. I had to pay my fare, so to speak, while we were crawling in the traffic.

JIM. She's anyone's.

KATE. Amusing with all the other drivers peering through the smog at me, on this truck driver's lap, but not very satisfying.

NELL. Pornography!

KATE. So you can imagine that when I was finally sitting on the window seat waiting for the airplane to start for the States, I was ready for anything.

NELL. Not a photographer – a pornographer!

JAMES (*giving her a drink*). There you are.

KATE (*tasting*). This is almost neat gin.

JAMES. We all need a stiff one.

They laugh at his unintended joke.

JIM. At this moment I'm the luckiest man in the history of civilisation. In a room with the two women I desire most in the world –

KATE. And now, at last, I've come to the point –

JIM. - and both of them desire me and there's nothing in art or science or religion to compare with this –

KATE. Well, to cut a long story short, I've fallen head-over-heels in love.

Pause.

JAMES. Well, well –

JIM. No, Kate, don't say that, please –

ELEANOR. How nice for you!

NELL. And even nicer for me!

KATE. Right.

JIM. And don't keep saying 'right'.

KATE. Suddenly there was this beautiful guy asking if he could move my gear from the seat next to mine –

NELL. Poor James!

She approaches him as he stands smiling and sipping his drink.

KATE. Then I realised bells were ringing.

JAMES. Was it a bomb scare?

KATE. What?

JAMES. Hi-jackers?

ELEANOR *laughs.*

KATE. No. In my head. Or wherever they ring.

JAMES. I was going to say 'Bells on a jumbo'!

KATE. My heart was jumping. I could hardly speak. I thought to myself 'My God, it's love'.

JIM. You told me you didn't *want* love.

JAMES. I thought they always put on soothing strings.

NELL. I must say I'm relieved.

ELEANOR. That must be wonderful.

KATE. Yes, it is, but sad to say they were also warning bells.

JIM. You didn't want another heavy scene.

NELL. Warning bells?

KATE. They were saying 'Go no further'. But I didn't read them then, I'm glad to say. For two weeks it was knock-out.

JIM. *We* could be knock-out.

KATE. LA, Vegas, San Francisco . . .

JIM. I've had no chance. The odd hour –

ELEANOR. Then why the warning bells?

JIM. But in Zurich –

KATE (*shrugs*). Oh, problems, problems –

NELL. Aaah!

JIM. Three days and three nights –

JAMES. What problems exactly?

KATE. None on my side.

NELL (*to* ELEANOR). Another married man.

ELEANOR. American?

KATE. English. Lives not far from here. I'm on my way to see him now and thought, as it sorts of concerns us all, I'd break my journey to let you know. I told him, 'let's take off, I'm yours'.

JIM. Be his, by all means, but mine as well.

ELEANOR. But he's not free?

KATE. He's got commitments.

ELEANOR. About your age?

KATE. No. Forty-ish.

NELL. I thought so.

KATE. Forty-five-ish.

NELL. Fifty-ish.

ELEANOR. And is he married?

KATE. Separated.

JAMES. Then what's the problem?

KATE. About to separate.

NELL. You mean you want to wreck *his* marriage?

KATE. Is that the end of the inquisition?

ELEANOR. Sorry. I was only asking.

> KATE *moves about, puts her glass on drinks shelf. The others wait.*

KATE. I didn't *choose* this to happen. I just fell in love.

JAMES. I never thought you were that romantic.

KATE. Eleanor doesn't think so either. She's cast me as a home-wrecker.

NELL. Oh, you can't stand disapproval, can you?

ELEANOR. *I* haven't cast you.

NELL. You want even the wives to love you.

KATE. You and Agnes both.

JIM. Don't compare my wife with Agnes.

ELEANOR. I'm not tolerant the way she was.

JAMES. You're tolerant in different ways.

> *He kisses her.*

ELEANOR. I told James he could go with you or stay with me.

JAMES. And put like that, I obviously stayed.

KATE. It was only a bit of fun. Now finished.

JIM (*going on his knees.*). Please, Kate.

KATE. And we're the best of friends again.

She takes ELEANOR*'s hand and reaches for* JAMES*'s. He takes hers. She impulsively kisses* ELEANOR.

Aren't we?

She kisses JAMES *on the cheek.*

JIM (*getting to his feet*). Insulting bitch.

NELL. She's enjoying this.

ELEANOR. You look very happy.

KATE (*shrugs*). I suppose that's being in love.

ELEANOR. I can just remember.

JAMES. I wouldn't know.

ELEANOR. He says he's never been in love.

KATE. You love each other.

ELEANOR. Oh, yes, but that's life – our daily bread. Being *in* love is different.

KATE. It's coming to life after having been dead.

JIM. Well, thanks.

NELL (*sympathetically*). Oh, James, she can't be worth it.

ELEANOR. James won't fall in love. He's got too much self-esteem.

KATE (*pitying*). Aah.

She again kisses him on the cheek.

JIM. If you peck me again like that, I'll bite a piece from your ear.

Doorbell rings.

ELEANOR. There's my student. Why don't you keep James company a bit?

NELL (*to her*). Don't rub salt in the wound.

KATE. I should really go.

JAMES. One for the road?

KATE. No, really, I mustn't keep him waiting.

ELEANOR *opens front door.* KATE *finishes drink.* NELL *stays halfway between hall and room.*

JIM. She's only punctual when it's new.

JAMES. Remember our first time – in the restaurant?

JIM. When you wanted me?

JAMES. You were punctual then.

KATE (*with a smile and a shrug*). Right.

JAMES. D'you know you use that word too often?

ELEANOR *admits young woman, takes her outer clothes and hangs them.*

KATE. Which word?

JAMES. 'Right'.

KATE. I do?

JAMES. Absolutely.

KATE. Same with you and 'absolutely'.

She goes to the hall. JAMES *and* JIM *follow.*

The WOMAN STUDENT*'s gone into the music room. She starts limbering up her voice with scales.*

KATE *meets and kisses* ELEANOR.

KATE. Let's make a date to go shopping.

ELEANOR. Yes, let's.

KATE. I'm sorry for any pain I caused you.

ELEANOR. All over now. Forgotten.

They embrace.

NELL. Should I be grateful? I don't know. He looks like death.

JIM. Love another man by all means but that doesn't mean I'm suddenly repulsive. How about my letter? Zurich?

KATE. I'll ring you.

ELEANOR. Do.

She goes to the music room and almost at once the piano begins to assist the STUDENT *in her scales.*

JAMES. Did you have a coat?

KATE. Yes.

JAMES (*getting it*). There's quite a chill in the air tonight. Winter coming.

NELL. Poor James fell for your sex act. I almost did myself tonight.

JIM. My life's ending as abruptly as it began – how many weeks ago?

JAMES (*helping her on with the coat*). Here we are.

NELL. But of course, you're really a romantic. Promiscuous people always are.

JIM. Kate, please . . .

He kisses her neck, goes on his knees before her.

JAMES. Did you get my letter?

KATE. It was nice of you to ask, but, well, you see how things are.

JIM. No, I don't.

JAMES. Absolutely.

KATE. We'll see each other soon. At Private Views.

JAMES. Why did you do it like this?

KATE. This was the best way.

She kisses him quickly and goes by the front door.

JIM (*following her, shouting*). I didn't know you wanted love. I'll say I love you. I'll do anything.

JAMES *closes the front door. NELL goes to join ELEANOR in the music room.*

Chorus: 'He trusted in God' from 'Messiah'.

Lights on upper level.

Private View begins, exactly as in Act One, but now the photographs are of sexual acrobatics.

JAMES *goes up the stairs and reveals a closer view of the coupling.* GUESTS *loudly approve, clap, whistle, etc. He reveals another, the face of Bernini's Saint Teresa. Laughter and ribald comments. He gestures for the* GUESTS *to follow him and leads them downstairs. They make themselves at home in the living room while* JAMES *fetches the Christ painting. At the same time* ELEANOR *comes from bedroom in nightgown, wanders along balcony, looking over at the* GUESTS, *trying not to be seen.*

JAMES *puts up the Christ and the reaction is as though this were the most obscene picture of all. Among the crowd we now distinguish* KATE, AGNES *and a* MAN *who might be Albert. He caresses them in turn.*

As ELEANOR *sees this,* JAMES *notices her and points her out to the crowd. She cowers but he calls her down and she hesitantly descends. He introduces her and they all applaud.*

ELEANOR *now takes over the lecture as* JAMES *goes into the crowd of onlookers, now waiting for* ELEANOR *to begin. But she's only concerned with* JAMES *and tries to see who he's with.*

There is a YOUNG WOMAN *behind the crowd and he stands behind her, caressing her breasts, kissing her hair and neck as she faces* ELEANOR, *listening.*

KATE, AGNES and the ALBERT MAN *begin catcalling for* ELEANOR *to start. This is taken up by others. Someone takes a flash photo, another plucks at the skirt of her nightdress to lift it. She covers herself and tries to move towards* JAMES *and the* GIRL *but they won't let her and* KATE *and* AGNES *both embrace her, kiss her, restrain her.* JAMES *has got some of the* GIRL*'s clothing off and is pulling her down on the floor.*

The crowd gather to watch this and surround them. ELEANOR *at last gets free and reaches this circle, pulling them away, fighting through. She reveals* JIM *with the half-dressed girl, kissing her body. Flash of camera.*

He is amused by ELEANOR*'s appearance and points at her nightdress. The* GIRL *is hidden by the crowd. They all exit through the various doors.* JIM *is the last to go.*

The pictures upstairs go as they came. JAMES *comes from the bedroom in pyjamas and dressing gown. Chorus ends and lights change.*

ELEANOR *in living room.* JAMES *coming downstairs.*

ELEANOR. Then suddenly it was in this room and I was up there trying to hide and you called me down in my nightdress to talk about the Christ painting –

JAMES. It was a nightmare. We all have nightmares. We don't have to spend the rest of the night going over –

ELEANOR. Meanwhile – at the back of the crowd you were taking off her clothes.

JAMES. Whose clothes? Kate's?

ELEANOR. No, it's not Kate. I know that. Someone else.

JAMES. Listen, will you believe me? There isn't anyone else. There never has been anyone else. Only her.

ELEANOR. How can I believe you? Ever again?

JAMES. Are you trying?

ELEANOR. You *lied* to me. You broke our trust.

JAMES. You lied to *me!* Over Albert.

ELEANOR *does not speak.*

By your own admission. How do I know that was the only time? Shall I make you some tea?

ELEANOR. Just get me a glass of mineral water.

JAMES *goes off.*

ELEANOR. Albert was nothing, I told you. I didn't change because of that. You didn't even notice. It's you who's changed.

JIM *comes back with mineral water, wearing pyjamas.*

JIM. *I* haven't changed.

ELEANOR. Not changed, no. Become hidden. I hardly recognise you any more. Abstracted, irritable. All you want to do is sleep. You lie there snoring and when at last I drift off I dream I'm singing an aria in the wrong key while you and Albert and Kate and Agnes sit in the front row –

JIM. Of course all I want to do is sleep when every night is spent picking over the same old entrails –

ELEANOR. You nod off over a book, in front of the TV, during concerts –

JIM (*over*). – looking for the same bad omens –

ELEANOR. – sleep is your way of getting through. Or is she so demanding you can't even keep awake?

JIM. Who? Who's 'she'? Kate?

ELEANOR. Not Kate, no. I know that's over –

JIM. There's no one else.

ELEANOR. Then why does so much of your work these days take you away from home?

JIM. So much?

ELEANOR. Two days a week at least.

JIM. Most men are away for five –

ELEANOR. You're not most men.

JIM. All right. I feel the need to get away. Nowadays, if there's a choice, I work at a gallery instead of here, *yes* –

ELEANOR. And when I ring you aren't there.

JIM. *Once* I wasn't there. I was running in the park. You won't even allow my jog on the common any more.

ELEANOR. I'm frightened alone.

She is crying. He embraces her and holds her.

ELEANOR. You never used to go away. We spent most of our lives together.

JIM. I've tried to persuade you that was wrong.

ELEANOR. You never wanted to go outside *then.*

JIM. How d'you know?

ELEANOR. You never *said.*

JIM. I should have. Variety is an aphrodisiac. Our married friends spend whole days apart. Without accounting. People need that freedom and privacy –

ELEANOR. *I* don't. You *didn't.*

JIM. Well, you were an untiring wife and mother. I worked hard to keep the family. Where many of our friends chanced their arms, took selfish risks with their children's futures, blew the lot on weekends away and sometimes tried a change of partner –

ELEANOR (*over this*). You didn't *want* that –

JIM (*not pausing*). – you and I made the long sure haul with no surprises. And one day we looked around to find our children gone. And you particularly were at the stage of life when every woman undergoes an inevitable change –

ELEANOR. Oh, no!

JIM (*angrily*). What?

ELEANOR. Not the change of life?

JIM. Whether you like the fact or not, my dear, you've reached the age when women suddenly . . .

ELEANOR. Go mad. Yes?

JIM. Can't feel the ground beneath their feet.

ELEANOR *shakes her head.*

ELEANOR. They go mad. *I'm* going mad. I feel it. What shall I do?

JIM. It isn't madness, love. It's an unwillingness to change.

ELEANOR. You keep on about change. But into what? A princess? A frog?

JIM. First you accept the need to. Then you find out. It's a question of bend or break at times. (*Leads her towards the stairs.*) Not only individuals but whole nations. Families are little countries. If they can't change they die. That last time Kate was here, for instance, you and I had accepted the thought of a sexual trio.

ELEANOR. It's always this. When you say 'change' you mean I must get used to the thought of –

JIM. Will you let me finish?

ELEANOR. Not if all you have to say is –

JIM. I am trying to help you.

ELEANOR. Then tell me what to do!

JIM. I hesitate to suggest this but I'm desperate –

ELEANOR. *You're* desperate?

JIM. I think we should get some outside help.

ELEANOR. Doctors?

JIM. I don't like it either but –

ELEANOR. Both of us.

JIM. Both of us, right. But first of all, you. Would you like me to arrange a check-up with Michael at the Middlesex? A physical first and if that's all right and you're still depressed, I dare say he'll be able to put you on to some other department.

ELEANOR. Us. Not me.

JIM (*gently*). It's you that's having the nightmares.

ELEANOR. It's you that brought them on.

JIM. The doctors may not agree. In fact, it may be best if you don't mention that business with Kate at all . . . they'd seize on that.

They've reached the upper landing now and go into the bedroom.

A slow chorus from the Matthew Passion.

A DOCTOR enters leading NELL. He speaks to her kindly, offers a chair on which she sits. He sits near her, opens a notebook, asks a question, she shakes her head, answers. We hear none of this, until the music ends.

NELL. No, the nightmares only started recently. As long as we had one daughter left at home, I felt useful but James had begun to think he'd given up too much of his life to the family. When the last one left it seemed to mark the beginning of freedom for the two of us. So I looked around for him but found he was occupied elsewhere. Out to lunch. No one home. I saw there was no home at all, except me. And half the time I was out to lunch myself. Dozing through a Passion. One day in rehearsal I found myself in tears when we sang 'Deliver me from the lion's mouth, call to me lest the bottomless pit shall swallow me . . . ' Not tears for the dead or mankind in general but for myself – I'd sung them for years without thinking and now I realised that behind the noble Latin noise there was a meaning for me . . . my day of wrath was coming . . .

Music again. The DOCTOR moves across behind her, reading the notes he's made. She turns to listen to him and, as he stands centre, lights come up slightly on the living room and JIM comes in with the GIRL from ELEANOR's nightmare by the front door. She looks around as though she's never seen the house before. Music ends.

It isn't fair to James, he spends hours of every day alone with a painting . . . when he comes back into the world he wants a sexy girlfriend, not a mental case, a woman whose true self is screaming with despair . . .

DOCTOR *has listened, now crosses to the side, making a note.* NELL *keeps her eyes on the living room, where* JIM *leads the* GIRL *to the stairs, caressing her as they climb* . . . if this is the change of life, I'd like some pills to regulate the chemistry . . . help me sleep. Are there any pills to banish daydreams?

JIM *and the* GIRL *continue along the balcony into the bedroom. The* DOCTOR *nods, writes and gives* NELL *a prescription. Music resumes.* DOCTOR *asks her another question.*

ELEANOR *has come from the side to join* NELL.

ELEANOR. . . . not always in the same place, no. But always the same girl. A junior partner in this gallery . . . he finds any excuse to go there . . . I think he sometimes has her in our house . . . he leaves the windows open but enough of the scent still hangs about . . . I know he's up to something, he's so remote . . .

NELL. He's always been a distant person. He was an only child, his parents spoilt him.

ELEANOR. They brought him up to believe in a life based on: take and it shall be given unto you.

NELL. So he finds love a mystery. He doesn't know what the word means. He says: why call affection, lust, belief in God, care for children, etcetera, by one word?

ELEANOR. We all recognise red, orange, yellow, blue, green and violet but we don't call them white just because they all become that when they're mixed together. He's trained himself to be precise about colours.

Music. Lights change. NELL *gets up and moves to the clothes cupboard by the front door. She takes out a coat.* JAMES *comes from the kitchen, doesn't see* NELL, *looks at his watch, looks upwards at the balcony as though guessing*

where she is. ELEANOR *sits in the chair near the*
DOCTOR. *She turns to the* DOCTOR *and speaks silently.*
JAMES *moves towards* NELL, *sees her. Music ends.*

JAMES. Ah! You off now?

NELL. Yes.

JAMES. So am I. For a walk on the common. I did tell you.
Possibly half an hour but it could be longer.

NELL. I didn't ask how long you'd be.

JAMES. If I undertake to be back within forty-five minutes,
would that be acceptable?

NELL. Take as long as you like. I'll be out the whole
afternoon, as you know. At the doctor's.

JAMES (*putting on his coat*). Tearing me apart?

NELL. He doesn't tear you apart.

ELEANOR (*to* DOCTOR). He resents it if I say we've talked
about him.

JAMES (*shrugs*). He says I'm treating you badly.

NELL *looks in a glass, repairs her makeup, sits to do so.*

JAMES, *behind her, looks at his watch.*

ELEANOR. Doesn't like me seeing you at all, in fact.

NELL. He's only trying to help.

JAMES. By moralising about my behaviour? I thought shrinks
weren't meant to allocate blame.

NELL. He's not a shrink. He's a clinical psychiatrist.

JAMES. Well, I hope he can be of some help.

ELEANOR. It smacks of the church, he says, employing a
professional to listen to our secrets. It means we've lost
faith in human intercourse.

JAMES *moves towards the front door.*

NELL. Are you walking across the common towards the
station? Let's stroll across together.

JAMES. I'm going the other way.

ELEANOR. I'm sure he doesn't mean to be cruel.

JAMES. If I come with you. I'd only have to walk all the way back before I could start my walk.

NELL. Yes, of course.

She has joined him at the front door, which he opens.

ELEANOR. We can't blame him for having a selfish nature.

JAMES (*kissing her*). See you later.

NELL. This incident as I left to come here gives you some idea what I mean. He set off positively enough, it's a chilly day, but I couldn't help seeing how soon he slowed down and seemed to be hovering. I didn't look back till I reached the main road near the station. Our house is easy to see from there and I took in something with half a mind that only really dawned when I was halfway here in the train. Our car had gone.

KATE *and* ELEANOR *enter with* SHOP ASSISTANT *and go into the dress shop and start trying on the nightdresses.*

KATE. So you think he'd gone off in the car to see that girl?

ELEANOR. But the doctor suggested James had got into the car to give me a lift.

KATE. And hadn't found you?

ELEANOR. That was his suggestion.

KATE. Sounds reasonable.

ELEANOR. A belated kindness, yes it does. He's a belated kind of man. Except that when I got back two hours later the car still wasn't there and nor was he.

KATE. What did he say when he did come in?

ELEANOR. Showed me the paints and brushes he'd been to buy. Trouble is the supplier's only ten minutes away.

KATE. If I were you I'd turn a blind eye. He feels spied on, you can learn nothing, he can lie. It's useless. Somewhere

I heard this great saying: Love isn't 'where've you been?' it's 'hello'.

ELEANOR. That's all right for a sexy affair. But what about afterwards?

KATE. Does there have to be an afterwards?

ELEANOR. Marriage, for instance.

KATE *has been changing into the underwear.* NELL *is climbing the stairs, but mostly hidden in half light.*

KATE. Ah, well, I wouldn't know.

ELEANOR. You lived with Albert for five years.

KATE. Living with is different.

ELEANOR. Is it?

KATE (*displaying herself*). What d'you think?

ELEANOR. It's very you.

NELL (*appearing*). How could James have touched that repulsive flesh?

ELEANOR. Is that the kind of thing your lover likes?

KATE. Right.

ELEANOR. I should buy it then.

KATE *still considers herself in the glass.*

ELEANOR's *trying on the negligée.*

NELL. You're an anthology of all James said he hated. Your smell, your complexion, the texture of your hair –

KATE. Trying on new clothes is life's greatest pick-me-up.

ELEANOR. Pick-me-up? I thought you were in love.

KATE (*shrugs*). Love's never easy. Unlike sex.

ASSISTANT *shows in another* WOMAN *to try on clothes.*

NELL. Sex easy? You're talking like a man. *For* a man. Talk to *me*.

KATE. Don't misunderstand. It's not easy deceiving wives, for instance. Especially when they're friends, like you. Not pleasant either.

ELEANOR. Then why go for middle-aged husbands?

KATE. They're wittier, more interesting, they've done something with their lives . . .

NELL. And aren't so demanding sexually?

KATE. And as lovers they take their time.

NELL. There you are. (*She goes.*)

KATE. This does nothing for me.

ELEANOR. The fact I'm suspicious he's got another woman doesn't mean he has, it just means I'm suspicious.

KATE. Do what I did with Albert. Make him suspicious of you.

ELEANOR. Mistrusting each other hasn't been our way.

KATE. It seems to be now.

ELEANOR. And whose fault's that?

KATE. Good question. Does anything particularly make you doubt him?

ELEANOR. Oh no, a million signs. Either he talks too little or too much. I find cigarette ends in the ashtray of the car. He makes calls from public boxes, while he's supposed to be jogging.

KATE. Don't tell me you spy on him?

ELEANOR. I can hear the ten-pence pieces clinking in his tracksuit pocket.

KATE. Now that looks more like a dirty weekend in Morocco, don't you think?

ELEANOR. Oh yes, and how about this for Florence?

KATE. For anywhere! I knew that was you somehow.

ELEANOR. But hell's bells, look at the price.

KATE. I'll take this one.

ELEANOR. Well I like it, but will my hubby?

KATE. I should think so.

ELEANOR. In that case I'll take it, because if she doesn't know, who does? How long will you be in Morocco?

KATE. Three days. Just long enough to freshen up my fading tan.

ELEANOR. We're having a week in Florence, though not till after Christmas. He'll be working on a Crucifixion in Switzerland for a few days soon and I wanted to go with him. He said it would be all work and no play.

KATE. It doesn't sound like a load of laughs, I must say.

ELEANOR. And I said. Are you taking your floozie instead? So to allay my suspicions, perhaps, he's booked this week by the Arno.

KATE. Well out of you and the floozie, I know who's got the best of the bargain.

ELEANOR. It's where we spent our honeymoon, Florence.

KATE. Out of Florence and Zurich, I know where I'd rather go.

NELL *and* AGNES *are found drinking in a bar. Men drink behind them.*

NELL. In the ordinary way I might not have noticed.

AGNES. How do you mean, in the ordinary way?

NELL. Before suspicion became a way of life.

ELEANOR. Did I say Zurich?

KATE. I didn't mention Zurich.

KATE. I'll pay for that in cash.

ELEANOR. I didn't say he was going to Zurich. I said Switzerland.

KATE. So?

ELEANOR. How did you come to know it was Zurich? Who's told you if it wasn't me? (KATE *walks off.*) Don't think you can just walk off –

AGNES. I thought you knew it was still going on.

ELEANOR. Kate. Did you hear what I said? Kate, wait for me.

AGNES. You must be the last person in London to find out.

NELL. She told me there was another man.

AGNES. One other?

NELL. One special man she met in America and fell in love with.

AGNES. Is that what she said? Well, it didn't last long. He was the usual middle-aged man with the usual wife but with one unusual feature – he preferred the wife to Kate. After a week or two he wrote and told her so. Then she went back to yours.

NELL. Why didn't you tell me?

AGNES. They were at Private Views together, sales at Sotheby's.

NELL. I knew there was someone, I never suspected her.

AGNES. What did she say when you caught her out?

NELL. Walked straight from the shop and jumped into a cab. You were the only person I could turn to.

AGNES. Eleanor, my love, my poor love . . .

NELL. I was afraid it was only in here. They'd convinced me I was going mad.

AGNES. Who had?

NELL. The doctors.

AGNES. Were they all men?

NELL. Yes

AGNES. The bastards are everywhere.

She looks round about at the MEN *drinking in the bar.*

NELL. They said it was the menopause.

AGNES. I'd heard he'd sent you to the shrink. The same one Albert sent me to.

NELL. Oh God!

AGNES. Their old chum Michael at the Middlesex sends all the psychologically battered wives to him.

NELL. James even pretended he didn't like me going there.

AGNES. One way or another we all get screwed. Eleanor, love, it's time you listened to the hooker's warning. Don't take it lying down.

NELL and AGNES *go off with the revolve.* JAMES *enters into the living room while the revolve is moving. He brings the Christ painting with him and speaks to it.*

JAMES. I've inspired love. I'm an unemotional man who's inspired a passion in my partner. And I needn't tell *you* what passion means. Suffering, self-inflicted torture, masochism, all that's holy. Like that exquisite depiction of a bleeding corpse that's waiting for me in Zurich. By day I'll patch it up, repair the blood and wounds where they've been knocked around over the years, but every night I'll fuck as though life depended on it. Which of course it does.

The doorbell rings. JAMES *answers it. A porter from the gallery delivers a new painting and collects the restored Christ.* JAMES *takes the new painting into the kitchen.*

The opening of the Lachrymosa from Mozart's Requiem. ELEANOR *enters at the front door with* NELL. *She sits sadly looking at the nightdress she's bought, while the music continues and fades.*

NELL. All right, is it decided, do we tell him to go?

ELEANOR. And if he does?

NELL. We must learn to forget him.

ELEANOR. I can't forget him, he's half my life.

NELL. Imagine him dead, then you'd have to. Tell him he's free to go to Zurich but not come back, or stay with me and give her up, but no more lies.

ELEANOR. All right.

NELL. And don't let him dodge again, he'll fog the issue if he can. It's in his interest to keep you both.

ELEANOR. I said all right.

JAMES (*entering with the new painting, now unwrapped*). Hullo love. How was your afternoon? You'll be glad to hear Old Killjoy's gone and look what they've brought instead. (*Shows her the painting – the canvas is uniformly yellow.*) It's going to be a swine matching this colour. That watermark there, you see. Swine. Been shopping?

ELEANOR. Yes, with Kate.

JAMES. How is she? Still head over heels in love?

ELEANOR. Oh yes.

JAMES. Is that what you've bought?

ELEANOR. A nightdress, yes, for the week in Florence.

JAMES. Must have cost the earth. Did Kate buy anything?

ELEANOR. A nightdress.

JAMES. Pretty tarty I'll bet.

ELEANOR. You'll be able to judge when you get to Zurich, only if you go don't bother coming back. I shan't be here, I know all about you and Kate. All I have to say is: if you go, you'll be leaving me.

Pause.

JAMES. I've never wanted to.

ELEANOR. Is that because she isn't any good in bed? That's what you said last time you finished with her. Not sensual.

JAMES. Not sensual the way you are, no. Something a bit implausible. Sexy without sensuality.

ELEANOR. Sexy? I see.

JAMES. Automatic. The price of changing partners so often is that you have to become a soloist.

ELEANOR. You love her. You're describing her with love. Whenever you've had me lately you've talked about her immediately after. Oh Christ, that should have told me.

JAMES. I don't know what's meant by love. I never have. What I feel for her is sexual attraction. Pure and simple.

ELEANOR. That's what men want to hear. Pornography. No periods, no pregnancies, no growing fond. No consequences. Violence without bruises.

JAMES. It's a physical act. It can be at its best between two people who don't even know each other's names.

ELEANOR. You've known each other's names for years.

JAMES. We've tried not to let that matter. We enjoy it.

ELEANOR. She enjoys the power she has over you and indirectly over me.

JAMES. She hasn't any power over me.

ELEANOR. Then give her up. You can't. You went on seeing her after you swore you wouldn't.

JAMES. I had to swear.

NELL *comes from bedroom in nightdress. Followed by* JIM *in pyjamas.*

JIM. I *had* to swear. You put a gun to my head.

NELL. I offered you a choice.

JIM. All or nothing.

NELL. Her or me.

JIM. You knew I wouldn't give you up.

NELL. You love her, why shouldn't you? She's young, available –

JIM. I don't know what's meant by love. Except pain and trouble and ownership. But you and I have been together twenty-five years – daughters, a string of flats and houses, annual holidays, narrow scrapes.

NELL. You make me sound like a family album. Whereas for her you feel desire, fascination . . .

JIM. I enjoyed the newness of her, yes. The flattery, the danger. At a time our life had grown secure and predictable, she brought back drama, looks across crowded rooms.

JAMES. Whenever I saw men touch her, I was elated because I'd been there.

ELEANOR. All the other ageing husbands?

NELL. Not to mention arms dealers, property speculators, drug pushers and journalists.

JIM. Abusing her won't help –

ELEANOR (*to* JIM). That's not abuse. That's fact. She's essentially uncreative.

NELL. A parasite among parasites.

JAMES. So am I.

ELEANOR (to JIM). She'll never finish that book she's started.

NELL. She lacks the stamina.

JIM. There are too many books in the world already. Not to mention paintings and passions and plays.

JAMES. Too much of everything. Too many chairs and tables.

JIM. And curtains and carpets.

JAMES. Too much of this clutter.

He goes about, throwing down books, cushions, magazines . . .

ELEANOR. He didn't throw anything fragile.

NELL. I noticed that.

JAMES. I can't. I'm too inhibited.

JIM. But she's got something I somehow never had – youth and independence.

NELL. I had that once before you turned me into a bourgeois wife, suffocated me with apparatus because it suited you.

JIM. Then throw it all off, be young again. She can help us. You must admit bed's been much better lately.

JAMES. The new flavour helped me relish the old.

ELEANOR. The old?

NELL. Get me a vodka.

JAMES. She belongs to another generation – free of convention, independent . . .

NELL. Hah!

JAMES. One of the people my generation wanted to create.

JIM. The freedom we championed is the air they breathe.

NELL. Her freedom's based on daddy's tax dodges.

JAMES. She parks on double yellow lines, she walks straight to the head of queues, she grabs what's going.

ELEANOR. In other words, disregards the morality you've always lived by.

JAMES. I've been very moral, yes.

ELEANOR. So go to her! What's keeping you here?

JIM. You.

NELL. An old flavour?

JIM. This!

NELL. A prison!

JIM. Eleanor, love, time is running out. You and I have twenty, twenty-five years if we're lucky, slowing down like a rusty old motor until one day we stop forever. So this is probably my last chance and where's the harm? It's marvellous being a lover. More thrilling than war and warmer than sunshine. My only regret is hurting you so why can't you allow me this flash of happiness before the void?

NELL. You can't have both.

JIM. Why not? I mean that: why not?

NELL. Because I won't be second best. Why should you expect it? A housekeeper whose husband keeps his love and desire for another woman.

JIM. It's half past two in the morning. If you want me to get on with my moral working life tomorrow . . .

NELL. I don't –

JIM. You'll have to let me get some sleep.

He goes into bedroom.

NELL. It's over, James. We're finished.

NELL *takes pills from handbag and then goes to the stereo and puts on a rock-record full blast. She goes off to the kitchen.*

JAMES. This is a game.

ELEANOR. A game?

JAMES. You must learn to play.

ELEANOR. You're a baby, James, you want to have your cake and eat it.

JAMES. When I was a young man cake was rationed.

JIM *comes from bedroom and down the stairs, running.* JAMES *and* ELEANOR *watch. He gets to the player and takes off the record with a violent screech of skidding stylus.*

NELL *reappears from kitchen carrying a plastic bag full of laundry, which she tips in a heap on the floor.*

JIM. You surely don't want the neighbours to suffer because you and I – what's this?

NELL. Your lover's laundry.

JIM. What?

NELL. She had so much to do before her dirty weekend I offered to do it for her.

JIM. You what?

NELL. She put it in my car and I was going to drop it off next time I went to the doctor –

JIM. You should never have made such an offer.

NELL. But now you can give it to her when you catch the plane to Zurich.

ELEANOR. I thought she was a friend. And Agnes, too. You haven't even left me any girlfriends.

NELL throws articles of KATE's laundry at JIM, who tries to pick them up and return them to the bag.

NELL. These childish socks! This sequinned blouse! These frilly knickers! Hasn't she got filthy taste?

JIM. She's different, that's all.

NELL (*showing him her clothes*). You don't agree? You don't agree that's awful?

JAMES. Yours isn't the only way of dressing.

JAMES helps him clear up.

NELL (*to* JIM). A year ago you would have.

JIM. You shouldn't have done this –

NELL. Now you can only think of the times you took them off, I suppose – revealing that repulsive flesh of hers –

She attacks him with her fists, pounding at his chest and shoulders as he turns away to avoid her blows. He falls down and she kicks at him with her bare feet.

JAMES and ELEANOR watch in silence till she tires.

JIM. All right, you win. I'll go tomorrow. You won't be happy till I do. Tonight I'll sleep in another room and tomorrow I'll go. Later we'll sort out what to do about the paintings in my workshop . . . and the rest of it . . .

NELL. Yes.

Pause. They stand, exhausted.

JIM. Is that all right?

NELL. It's what you want.

Pause.

JIM. If you say so.

She goes upstairs. He starts picking up KATE*'s clothes from about the room, stuffs them into the bag.*

NELL *goes to the small WC and pours a glass of water, takes out the bottle of pills.*

ELEANOR. Go and help.

JAMES. It had to come, some push from someone.

NELL *is swallowing the whole bottle of pills, one by one, with water.*

JIM. We can't go back to the old life now.

ELEANOR. Only thinking about yourself.

JAMES (*pointing upstairs*). You mean you're not?

JIM. I don't want to leave her but life's so short.

JAMES (*to* ELEANOR). Look how suddenly Albert died.

JIM. What's kindness and decency and loyalty going to matter then?

JAMES. In the endless night when no one screws!

ELEANOR (*to* JAMES). Why didn't you guess what was happening?

JAMES. Because I'd never do that. Not for you or Kate or the children.

ELEANOR. Help us someone.

JAMES (*in the hall, looking up*). I lack the passion.

JIM *takes the bag of clothes to the kitchen.*

NELL *finishes the pills and comes to upper landing, drowsily. She sits on the top step.*

Pause.

JIM *returns to hall, looks up to see* NELL *sitting there.*

JIM. Ah, listen, why don't you stay in our bed? I'll have Ruth's old room. That will give us a night's sleep, or what's left of it. We'll need clear heads tomorrow to discuss the question of our joint account and the credit cards and how to divide the spoils. You'll need the car, I'll use the train. Or perhaps I can take one of the girls' old bikes. You'll have to pass on messages from the answering machine.

ELEANOR. You looked free at last.

JAMES. I was frightened.

JIM. See how we've become an institution? The house, the girls, the pension fund –

JAMES. A whole political structure.

ELEANOR. Blow it up. Thousands do.

JAMES. I tried. You saved it all.

NELL. I should have thought of this sooner. So much simpler for everyone. You could keep this place, she could move in with you . . .

JIM. What? You're rambling rather –

NELL. And I'd be free of both of you. All of it . . .

JIM. Well, when I go you will be, yes . . .

He is at the bottom of the stairs.

NELL. I love my children . . . tell them I love them.

She stands, loses balance and falls down several stairs till JIM *saves her.*

JIM. What's the matter with you?

NELL. The sleeping tablets.

JIM. No. Oh, no.

He holds her face and looks at it. Her eyes are closed.

How many?

NELL. Mmmm?

JIM. How many did you take?

NELL. The whole lot.

JIM. How many's that?

NELL. I don't know.

JIM. Think.

NELL. I stopped counting at thirty.

JIM. Stand up. Come on, stand.

He pulls her to her feet and unsteadily helps her up the stairs and into the WC. He lets her collapse on her knees in front of the lavatory and then sticks two fingers into her mouth. She makes retching sounds and he holds her head over the pedestal but she does not vomit. He tries again. She protests and tries to push his hand away.

JIM. You've got to. Come on.

ELEANOR *and* JAMES *are standing downstage looking up at* NELL *and* JIM *as* NELL *again makes retching noises.*

ELEANOR. What did you feel for me?

JAMES. At this moment? Let me think . . .

ELEANOR. Love?

JAMES. Christ, no! Hadn't we had enough of love? It was love that brought us to that!

He points to the scene above.

ELEANOR. What then?

JAMES. Amazement, I think.

ELEANOR. Why?

JAMES. That you could have tried to take the only life you'll ever have.

NELL *retches.*

JIM. That's a good try . . . but I don't think you've brought up anything . . . come on now . . . up on your feet . . .

NELL. Leave me alone . . .

He helps her as they leave the lavatory for the stairs.

ELEANOR. Why amazed? I'd lost your love. I'd nothing to live for.

JIM. We're going downstairs to the doctor . . . try to concentrate on walking . . .

JAMES. I thought we agreed we'd never loved.

ELEANOR. But now I realised we had.

NELL *tries to sit on stairs but* JIM *keeps her walking.*

JIM. Don't depend on me.

ELEANOR. All the time. Without knowing it.

JIM. That's a good girl.

ELEANOR. In this game, as you call it, I had no cards left to play.

JIM (*as they reach the lower level and the sofa*). Now where's the telephone? Tell me where it is.

ELEANOR. Except my life.

JIM. What's the doctor's number? Try to remember, head up, tell me the doctor's number.

ELEANOR *goes.* JAMES *moves after her some paces, speaking to her.*

JAMES. More than amazement, I felt anger. That you'd yet again held a gun to my head.

NELL. . . . The front of the book.

JIM. I know, but try to remember it. Concentrate.

He finds the number and dials while NELL *mumbles.*

JAMES (*returning to look at NELL*). ' I'll show you how much I love you . . . I'll die for you. Which may well ruin the rest of *your* life too . . . '

JIM. James Croxley here . . . oh, ambulance, please.

JAMES. Of course I prayed to the God I don't believe in that you wouldn't die.

JIM. Very urgent, yes, I'm afraid my wife's taken an overdose . . .

JAMES. Or survive with a damaged brain.

JIM. Over thirty. We're not really sure.

JAMES. I imagined you dead and as a hopeless cripple and none of that made me love you either.

JIM. What can I do until you get here?

JAMES. You'll never know this, Eleanor, but as I saw you lying there I hated you. For the first and last time.

JIM. All right. Thank you.

Puts down phone. Pulls NELL *to her feet.*

Come on, my dear –

JAMES. No pangs of guilt. Why should I? It wasn't my fault.

JIM. Now make an effort to stand upright.

JAMES. I don't want anyone to die for love of me.

He goes. Lights on JIM *and* NELL. *He has moved her to the stairs.*

JIM. We're going to go up there again now. Then we may come down again because you mustn't fall asleep before they get here.

Gets her to stairs and up they go again.

He says you'll be all right. It takes half an hour for barbiturates to get into the bloodstream. So, though it was a stupid thing to do, you weren't in any danger as long as you let me know in time. Which you did.

On upper level he walks her along, back and forth.

Someone told me most women who try to kill themselves don't succeed. Whereas most men do. Did you know that?

NELL. Who?

JIM. What?

NELL. Who told you that? Was it Michael at the Middlesex?

They go as the lights go.

Christmas music. A choir singing 'In the Bleak Midwinter'.

Lights come up slowly on living room. Outside snowy scenes. A YOUNG WOMAN (JAMES and ELEANOR's daughter) is decorating with tinsel and paper chains. ELEANOR comes from bedroom doing the same as on the upper level. A YOUNG MAN (their son-in-law) brings a Christmas tree in a tub from the kitchen and stands it in the living room. Begins to add bells, tinsel etc.

ELEANOR has come down and her daughter goes to the kitchen. JAMES comes from there with the finished yellow canvas. JIM follows. The women come back with trays of drinks and glasses. They all make welcoming and cheerful sounds as the music continues behind. JAMES leans the picture against a sofa and they all take glasses of wine. They raise their glasses as the music ends.

ELEANOR. Happy Christmas.

THREE OTHERS. Happy Christmas.

They drink. NELL comes on upstairs and watches from the balcony.

JAMES. And the painting's finished.

ELEANOR. Oh, well done.

JAMES. As near as I can get. That yellow was a swine to match. Acrylics are always tricky.

They look at the canvas.

ELEANOR. It looks exactly the same to me but I couldn't even *see* a stain.

They laugh.

How did you know it was there?

JAMES. It was there all right. Stood out a mile if you're used to looking at paintings.

NELL. You mean, like her?

ELEANOR. It may be philistine, but I always say I could do those paintings with a roller.

JAMES. I know you do.

ELEANOR. Now that you've done, you can give a hand here.

JAMES. Absolutely.

ELEANOR. We're a bit behind so hang some mistletoe and holly.

JAMES. Right.

ELEANOR. You and Robert can go and dress now. Your father and I can finish here.

The other two go upstairs and off to another room.

JIM. Dearest Kate, I picked up your latest letter from the gallery.

NELL. This isn't any good, is it? Nothing's settled, nothing's changed.

JIM. Eleanor's still got a way to go before I've nursed her back to health.

NELL. I offered you all I had but you couldn't respond.

JIM. She won't go back to the shrink. Several nights a week we're up all night . . .

NELL. Poor baby . . .

JIM. Obviously I can't risk hurting her so till she's well again we'll have to make do with letters.

NELL. You can't grow. You dream of change but when the chance comes you flirt with both.

JIM. And while yours are as hot as that, I shan't grumble . . .

Takes out air letter and reads it over.

NELL. You're not even promiscuous . . . it's always the same dream girl over Andover . . .

ELEANOR. How are you getting on with the mistletoe?

JAMES. What do you think?

ELEANOR. Well, it's sparing, isn't it?

JAMES. Is it?

ELEANOR. Minimal. Like the painting.

NELL. Like you. Minimal Man.

JAMES. Another bit of paganism swallowed up by Christianity. Let's try it, shall we?

They kiss. JIM *finishes reading* KATE'*s letter, goes back to his room.*

JIM. Getting your letter home nearly burnt a hole in my pocket.

NELL. But where are you? Out to lunch as usual.

JAMES. It seems to work.

ELEANOR. Yes?

NELL. No one home.

JAMES. I think we can make a go of it, don't you?

NELL. No.

ELEANOR. We can try.

JIM. I want you both but she wants all or nothing.

NELL. I want a lover, not an old friend.

ELEANOR. Now you've ruined my face and guests are due.

NELL. You can't do without all this. But I can. Change doesn't frighten me . . . .Once I'd lost your love there was nothing to keep me here. So goodbye.

JIM. Love's a terrible thing. It means whatever you want it to. So let's not either of us ever mention the word again.

NELL *goes off to the bedroom as* JAMES *comes back and puts on a record of 'In Dulce Jubilo', very joyous, and now there is no more dialogue.*

JIM *folds and seals his letter in the envelope.*

The doorbell rings as NELL *goes.* ELEANOR *comes from the music room and opens the door to* AGNES *and a* MALE FRIEND. *They embrace and warmly greet one another, talking above the music but unintelligibly.* JAMES *too greets them and gives them drinks. The* YOUNG COUPLE *come from the bedroom, dressed for a party, and join in.* AGNES *and her* FRIEND *go through a routine of removing outer clothes, which* ELEANOR *hangs in the cupboard.*

Again the doorbell rings. They all gesture to each other to answer the door. The YOUNG WOMAN *goes to admit two more* FRIENDS, *who take off coats, etc, embrace their hosts, accept drinks, look at Christmas tree.* JIM *has crossed to a place near the kitchen. He stands staring out at the audience while* JAMES *politely deals with his* GUESTS. *Again the bell rings and this time* JAMES *goes to admit a single* FRIEND.

NELL *appears from the bedroom, wearing her outer clothes and carrying a suitcase. She stares down at the party from there. As many* GUESTS *as possible have arrived and filled the stage before* JIM *closes his eyes and smiles. The doorbell rings but no one hears it. It rings on continuously till* JIM *crosses the room to the door.* NELL *comes downstairs and passes* ELEANOR, *who looks at her before returning to her* GUEST. JIM *opens the door to* KATE, *who enters in a fur coat and high-heeled shoes. He leads her through the part, leaving the door open.* NELL *goes by it, closing the door behind her.*

JIM *embraces* KATE, *unbuttons her coat, opens it and stares at her naked body beneath. He kneels before her and kisses her body.* JAMES *absently stares at the audience as* ELEANOR *chats to her* GUESTS. *The party goes on, the singing swells.*

Curtain.

Afterword

There have already been at least four published versions of this script in English alone. I foresee the sort of textual confusion so beloved of academics. Anyone interested in sorting this muddle is referred to an offprint of the *Bibliographical Society*, Sixth Series, Vol IX (December 1987), by Thomas Clayton. Include me out.

The play was first directed in 1981 by the late Mike Ockrent and again by him in 1984. In 2000, it has been revived at the Donmar Warehouse, a production that transferred to the Comedy. The present script retains the old stage directions and anyone reading it now and seeing the show will be able to compare my original intention with the new minimal version presented by director Michael Grandage and his designer Christopher Oram. They have laid bare the action, stripping it of distracting scenery and props, a decision I at first doubted, being so fond of Ockrent's productions. But they were right for this time and place. In the Donmar's dark cockpit, the actors were so close, so tangible, that an audience needed little else. I usually prefer (and write for) picture-frame stages, but this show has gone some way towards changing my mind.

When I stood behind the upper level to watch the play (or part of it, as my 72-year-old legs wouldn't take the whole two hours), I was reminded of another theatre, at Guy's Hospital in south London, where the director Michael Blakemore and I researched *The National Health*, a comedy set in a public ward. From domes in the ceiling, we watched a prostatectomy and something uterine, where the vulnerable bodies almost ceased to be human, only fleshy bags which, when opened, revealed gory confusions of inner organs that in those days were never seen in hospital dramas. Now such sights are commonplace on peak-hour TV and that old play would have to be radically rewritten. But we felt no revulsion at these sights. Only when the surgeons began dental or optical work and the faces were opened did I have to step outside for a smoke.

The comparison with pornography is obvious. Bodies may be beautiful but the heads are where pain and passion live, which turn into love (or hate). Voluptuous settings are less arousing than stony or metallic ones, emphasising the softness of flesh. There was a cold, clean sexiness in the surgical team's light clothing, in their precision, in the banter that relieved their concentration in our voyeuristic presence in the dome, just as, at the Donmar, an audience on three sides peered down into the lit arena at the dissection of adultery my play had become.

The enclosing audiences of these modern theatres are more congenial to generations raised on TV drama, the intimate views of faces and slight nuances of voice. This is why authors want their plays at such wraparound places, preferring Cottesloe to Lyttelton or Olivier. The play becomes the thing. What surprised me more was that, at the Comedy (Thomas Verity, 1881), yet another perspective appears. Extra walls now mask the wings and the actors enter and exit from both sides but not through the spectators. A symmetry gives an almost classical look to the bare staging. Distance lends formality.

Not only stages but audiences change. At the play's first appearance in 1981, the entry of the first doppelgänger was usually met by a sort of Mexican wave, as men asked women who this chap was that was invisible to everyone else on stage. More often than not, it *was* this way round – men mystified, women explaining. This time there's been no such confusion. Perhaps news has got around. Or (as I prefer to think) the play has at last found its time. We profited from previous productions and learnt to keep a little ahead of the audience but not too far. Though all the reviews described the initial idea of alter-egos, none bothered with the further jumps taken in Act Two (or the return to Square One in the final scene). The goalposts keep getting moved and, for the 1984 version, I moved them once too often, switching Eleanor and Nell for the last scene. As I left the theatre one night, a woman identified me to her friend who said, 'Then ask him what he means by the ending.' I knew what I meant but it was one move too far for first-time viewers. The present version reverts to my first. We have to make our meanings clear without becoming banal.

Peter Nichols